CONTEMPORARY FAMILY JUSTICE

POLICY AND PRACTICE IN COMPLEX CHILD PROTECTION DECISIONS

KIM HOLT

Foreword by Sir James Munby

Jessica Kingsley *Publishers*
London and Philadelphia

First published in 2016
by Jessica Kingsley Publishers
73 Collier Street
London N1 9BE, UK
and
400 Market Street, Suite 400
Philadelphia, PA 19106, USA

www.jkp.com

Library of Congress Cataloging in Publication Data
Names: Holt, Kim.
Title: Contemporary family justice : policy and practice in complex child
    protection decisions / Kim Holt.
Description: London ; Philadelphia : Jessica Kingsley Publishers, 2016. |
    Includes bibliographical references.
Identifiers: LCCN 2015046072 | ISBN 9781849056267 (alk. paper)
Subjects: LCSH: Custody of children--England--Psychological aspects. |
    Children--Legal status, laws, etc.--England. | Child welfare--Government
    policy--England. | Family social work--Law and legislation--England. |
    Custody of children--Wales--Psychological aspects. | Children--Legal
    status, laws, etc.--Wales. | Child welfare--Government policy--Wales. |
    Family social work--Law and legislation--Wales.
Classification: LCC KD779 .H65 2016 | DDC 346.4201/73--dc23 LC record available
at
http://lccn.loc.gov/2015046072

British Library Cataloguing in Publication Data
A CIP catalogue record for this book is available from the British Library

ISBN 978 1 84905 626 7
eISBN 978 1 78450 249 2

Printed and bound in Great Britain

Contents

Foreword

This is a very interesting, important, challenging and in places appropriately provocative book, which everyone involved professionally with the multi-faceted challenges of child protection would do well to read.

Much has been written about the family justice reforms implemented in April 2014. Much of this writing, valuable though it is, has taken a narrowly legal perspective and focused on the practice and procedures of the Family Court. Kim Holt takes a broader perspective and raises wider and more searching questions. Fundamentally, she suggests that the reforms to date are not enough, and in too many respects have not worked as their authors would have wished or, most important of all, as they should be working if the interests of both children and their parents are to be supported and their interests protected.

Our author raises uncomfortable questions about the pre-proceedings phase in care proceedings; about the limited visibility of children in the Family Court; about our handling of repeat removals of children from their parents; about the extent to which the combined pressures of the 26-week rule in care cases and judicial decision making in the Supreme Court and Court of Appeal are impacting – and, she suggests, impacting inappropriately and adversely – on social work practice; about the impact of austerity in general and legal aid changes in particular; and about much more.

I do not agree with all her conclusions, but that is not the point. The point is that she has identified challenging questions and articulated conclusions which we would all do well to ponder. We cannot afford to be complacent. We must, all of us, have the humility to recognise what is in need of improvement and the determination to do something – in truth, rather a lot – about it.

The changes in 2014, important though they were, did not mark the end of the road. There is much that remains to be done and indeed must be done if we are to meet our aspirations. I trust that when a new edition of this book appears in due course our author will be able to applaud the achievements of this ongoing process of reform and improvement.

Sir James Munby
President of the Family Division

Acknowledgements

This book has developed out of a series of lectures, papers, legal advice and research in response to changes to the family justice system.

I would like to include a special note of thanks to Professor Karen Broadhurst, with whom I started this journey in 2008 and who provided leadership in the Cafcass Project, and to all academic colleagues who were involved in the project; Dr Nancy Kelly, Dr Paula Doherty and Dr Emily Yeend.

I am deeply indebted to the support of Dr Nancy Kelly who has co-authored a number of papers, and who continues to provide ideas, support, guidance and patience.

To my daughter Amy who has provided unquestioning support, and my sister Tracey who inspires me. Thank you for your continued love and support.

Preface

Contemporary Family Justice: Policy and Practice in Complex Child Protection Decisions offers a unique lens on the legislation, policies and procedures for decision making in some of the most complex child protection cases.

Whilst the rhetoric of policy and legislation has been to ensure that the family justice system is responsive to the needs of children and their families when they are in crisis, in practice, responding to targets, timeframes and procedures for all front-line practitioners operating within the family justice system remains a priority.

The chapters in this book challenge our perceptions of decision-making processes in the most complex cases, and encourage the reader to think critically about government priorities in respect of children and their families who experience a range of vulnerabilities.

Furthermore, I invite the reader to consider the impact on children and their families of a shift towards remote control practice amongst all professionals in response to achieving timescales and targets, but without the necessary increase in resources.

The policy context in respect of family justice is complex and changing rapidly. In response, I have gone beyond focusing on the role of local authorities in relation to administrative procedures for child protection, and the role of agencies involved in public law cases, to offering a nuanced understanding of the role of the family justice system in both public and private law proceedings.

This book will assist all practitioners operating within the family justice system in gaining an understanding of the complexities of the political, legal and practice landscape of complex child protection decision making.

CHAPTER 1

Introduction

The Origin of Remote Control Practice

The Public Law Outline (PLO) (Ministry of Justice (MOJ), 2008) heralded a new era of a formal pre-proceedings process in respect of public law child care proceedings. The intention behind the protocol was to divert cases away from the courts and require local authorities to resolve disputes where safe and possible to do so within a formal pre-proceedings space.

Furthermore, the protocol was intended to ensure that cases were better prepared, with any disputed issues narrowed should a case proceed to court that would allow care proceedings to be resolved within a short timeframe. The PLO set in train the changes that were introduced with the Children and Families Act 2014, where a deadline for the completion of the majority of cases is set at 26 weeks.

The protocol is required to be used where a local authority has concerns that the threshold for care proceedings is met, but the risk to the child is not immediate. The protocol requires the local authority to send the parents a 'letter before proceedings', inviting them to a meeting to discuss its concerns. The letter entitles parents to legal aid so they can attend a meeting with a lawyer. The meeting is principally to share concerns about the welfare of the child and to agree a plan to divert cases away from court where it is safe and desirable to do so, or, where there is an assessment that the risk to the child is too high, an application to court should be made. It is envisaged that during this period any assessments required to inform the decision making of the local authority should be undertaken, rather than waiting to complete assessments when an application to court has already been made.

The rhetoric may indeed sound laudable, but the reality in practice is that this protocol highlights a growing trend in child protection practice towards what I describe as a 'remote control approach'. The courts and the local authority want to retain control of children and their families, but from a distance, with intervention highly prescribed, procedural and regulated – remote control. The rhetoric is bolstered by claims that new ways of working, whether within public law or private law proceedings, are concerned with avoiding delay, principally for children, as time is of the essence. However, as we shall see, an overarching theme in every chapter is on reducing resources and costs to the state. It may not be immediately apparent when thinking about child protection and family justice of the importance of private law proceedings when considering outcomes for children and their families. Private law proceedings are indeed extremely relevant, and the inclusion of a case study that will feature in each chapter may assist the reader in understanding the important relationship between public and private law proceedings.

Case study

Kelly (24) and Hassan (30) are married and have one child, Bertie, aged 12 months. Kelly's mother died from a drug overdose when she was nine, and she was looked after by her grandparents until she was 13 when Kelly was taken into care, as her behaviour had become increasingly challenging for her grandparents, who were in their late 70s. Kelly was reported as frequently going missing from home, and there was evidence of alcohol and drug usage from the age of 12.

The local authority accommodated Kelly for three years during which time she was regularly reported to the police as missing and there was concern expressed by the local authority with regards to an escalation of drug and alcohol usage. Kelly moved to her own accommodation when she was 16, and her social worker and grandparents continued to be concerned about her lifestyle, which was viewed as being chaotic, with reports to the police that Kelly was working as a prostitute to support her alcohol and drug usage. Kelly became pregnant at the age of 17 with Lucy, who was removed at birth – father not known. A year later Kelly became pregnant with her second child, Molly, who was also removed at birth – father not known.

Kelly met Hassan when she was 20 and they subsequently married a year later. Hassan was considered by Kelly's grandparents and the local authority as providing stability for Kelly. Hassan was successful as a self-employed entrepreneur and they enjoyed a comfortable home with a mortgage. When Kelly became pregnant with Bertie the local authority were satisfied that the previous risks were now reduced and Bertie was allowed to remain in the care of his parents.

Bertie is now 12 months old and the relationship between Kelly and Hassan has deteriorated. Hassan wants a divorce and the future in respect of Bertie is uncertain. Kelly has no independent source of income and there are concerns being raised by Hassan that Kelly has continued to use alcohol during their relationship. He is also concerned for the welfare of Bertie if he is to remain living with Kelly following their separation.

- As you read through this chapter, consider whether and how you would respond to this family.

- Consider the implications of decision making taking place within a pre-proceedings protocol for Bertie, Kelly and Hassan.

The impact of a system driven by the rhetoric of the 'timetable for the child'

In a contemporary climate of austerity, timescales, targets and protocols this book invites the reader to explore whether children and their parents are central and remain the priority for professionals and agencies within the current child protection system in England. Evidence suggests that achieving partnership working in the context of child protection has become increasingly elusive, particularly when parents are notified that the local authority are considering compulsory intervention to remove their children under the Children Act 1989 (Broadhurst and Holt, 2010). Recent changes to legislation, policy and practice introduced with the aim of achieving earlier decisions within the timeframe for the child are indeed commendable but there are consequences for both children and their parents. The aspirations of the Public Law Outline (2008) and (2014) are well rehearsed, but the changes that have been introduced with the modernization of the family justice system, alongside particular constructions of parenting, may be failing to recognize the potential of many parents. What would be the outcome if support is offered that is not merely packaged within a timeframe, and judgements made, if they cannot turn their lives around to care safely for their children within weeks.

Decision making and partnership

The principle of partnership working with parents to safeguard and promote the welfare of children is embedded within the Children Act 1989. Adopting an adversarial approach within the context of child protection rarely improves matters for the child and their family. Pivotal in ensuring that the best outcomes for children are achieved is policy and practice which aims to resolve matters in a fair, equitable and timely manner (Holt and Kelly, 2012b).

However, the state, in the guise of the local authority, is not a neutral umpire, arbitrating impartially between the courts and parents. Local authorities are perceived by parents to be a coercive power that aims to protect itself from invasion by both parents and parliament, who may seek to challenge them in the interests of another process (Parton, 2014b).

English law permits local authorities to make many decisions affecting children and their families without providing them with a hearing (Holt, 2014a). Local authorities have resisted pressures for legislation which would make the content of committee meetings available to the press and the public, thereby allowing the potential for the wielding of private power.

The impetus to move decision making in the context of child protection into an administrative rather than judicial arena is persuasive; engaging with families to achieve consensual solutions in an attempt to divert cases away from the court is desirable in achieving positive outcomes for children and reducing delay. However, for many families there is deep suspicion and mistrust of the local authority in terms of transparency, expertise and independence (Holt and Kelly, 2012a).

Despite consistent aspirations to improve the engagement of parents in the child protection process, studies continue to highlight difficulties in achieving those aims. There is a significant body of literature outlining the problematic nature of achieving consensual solutions; these are probed in some detail in Broadhurst and Holt (2010). Reasons for this are multiple, and include the difficulty of engaging with families and children with complex needs and varying levels of cooperation, the difficulties of multi-agency working and the constraints of economic and cultural resources. Achieving positive outcomes in family engagement when trying to divert cases away from the courts within the PLO is arguably more pivotal than ever in terms of the likely trajectory of child protection cases.

In the context of recent developments in child protection practice, commentators such as Broadhurst, 2009; Broadhurst and Holt, 2010; Shaw *et al.*, 2009; and White and Broadhurst, 2009 have suggested that on a purely practical level the reorganization of front-line services, and the implementation of a model of working that prioritizes the inputting of data over the rich analysis that comes from direct contact with children and their families, will inevitably result in disembodied forms of communication and a remote control approach – retaining power and control but with minimal levels of direct contact, which engender feelings of mistrust on the part of professionals, parents and children.

This issue is further highlighted in *The Munro Review of Child Protection: Final Report* (2011) where Munro notes that increasing rules, more detailed procedures and the over-reliance on information and communication technology systems has reduced the time available for direct *engagement* with families. Despite the intention of the PLO to effectively engage with families at a pre-proceedings stage, there appear to be far more bureaucratic and institutional obstacles to facilitating such engagement.

Notwithstanding the practicalities of local authorities engaging with families at all stages of the decision-making process, there is also the issue of the rights of participants to advice and representation. An aspect of Article 6 of the European Convention on Human Rights (ECHR) protects the right of everyone to 'a fair and public hearing' in the determination of their civil rights and obligations (*P, C and S v United Kingdom* [2002]).

If decision making in the most complex of cases is being moved increasingly to a pre-proceedings space, the need for good advocacy and independent legal advice and representation is crucial for families. Importantly, research suggests that parents can strike up positive relationships with their legal representatives even when relationships have broken down with the local authority (Brophy, 2006). Hence, it is important to ensure that representation provides parents with an important source of support, which can also facilitate dialogue between parents and the local authority.

It is probably too early to assert unequivocally that there is a duty to ensure representation or to define or describe the circumstances in which the duty may come into play. However, the introduction of the PLO with the formal statement of the right for parents to have legal representation at the pre-proceedings stage would seem to comply with the duty imposed by Article 6 to permit representation. This book examines how the erosion of legal aid, following the implementation of the Legal Aid Sentencing and Punishment of Offenders Act 2012, has in some areas of the UK resulted in the closure of many legal firms, restricting access to legal assistance, even if parents have the funds to pay privately for legal representation (Holt and Kelly, 2015c).

Furthermore, it is suggested that whilst the PLO may appear to be compliant with the ECHR there are issues in relation to the implementation of this intent. Arguably, there is significant contrast between the support and representation that is available both to the parent and, separately, to the child, when judicial decision making is involved and when the decision making is administrative. In court the child has the assistance of both a guardian and a professional advocate; in administrative procedures representation specifically for the child may be absent. The independent representation of children is essential to avoid conflating the needs and rights of parents and children. Given the impetus of the PLO to achieve diversion, the interim report of the Family Justice Review (March, MOJ, 2011b), highlighted the need for a pilot study to be undertaken to consider the role of the family court advisor being appointed at the pre-proceedings stage. A study is currently under way to explore the potential contribution of a guardian being appointed at the pre-proceedings stage specifically to represent the interests of the child. The final report of the Family Justice Review published on 3 November 2011 (MOJ, 2011a) makes reference to this research as ongoing. The challenge highlighted in the final report is to provide a system that is quicker, simpler, more cost-effective and fairer, whilst also continuing to protect children from risk of harm. The importance of effective engagement with parents at the pre-proceedings stage remains pivotal if we are to achieve a family justice system.

Although the PLO highlights the importance of representation for parents at the pre-proceedings stage, there is limited research that evaluates the effectiveness of representation in practice. Jessiman, Keogh and Brophy (2009) commented that the PLO (amongst other things) had not appeared to enhance parental capacity to benefit from legal advice at the pre-proceedings stage. Where parents had been involved with a local authority for some time, Jessiman *et al.* found they may be slow to access legal advice for a number of reasons, including their own vulnerability or limited capacity to understand the letter before proceedings, or their perception of legal representation as part of the system 'threatening' them and their families. Additionally, Jessiman and colleagues' respondents (members of the legal profession or guardians) noted that timescales between receiving the letter before proceedings and proceedings being issued may not be adequate to allow meaningful engagement with parents and, perhaps more fundamentally, that the investment by the local authority in the pre-proceedings work may be perceived as an intention to proceed.

Masson (2008) expressed concerns at that stage about the attempts to reduce legal costs in family work and raised serious concerns about fair access to justice. As she noted in relation to representation for families: 'Both the level of fees and the negative response to the reform process are likely to result in a reduction in the numbers of experienced solicitors doing this work' (2008, p.4). Furthermore, Masson asserts that a two-tier system may emerge, resulting in a local authority having a distinct advantage in terms of access to the most experienced legal advice and representation; and parents, in contrast, finding it difficult to locate an experienced representative is evidenced in *Re D (Non-Availability of Legal Aid)* [2014] (see Chapter 2). In this regard, the concerns raised by both Masson in 2008 and Jessiman *et al.* in 2009 in terms of the potential impact of changes to legal funding have come to fruition. It is evident that families don't have fair access to experienced legal representation at the important pre-proceedings stage. Unequal access to legal representation is likely to impact further on already problematic partnership working.

Relationships between practitioners and families need to be contextualized within the wider political, economic and social context. It is essential that we recognize the possible implications for families and service providers of the wider social welfare changes that were introduced by the UK coalition government (Featherstone *et al.*, 2011). Moreover, we must consider the continuing impact of public sector cuts upon the ability of the local authority, and social workers in particular, to ensure justice is achieved for children and families within a protocol that necessitates resources and financing. The cumulative impact of austerity measures within the local authority and changes to legal funding will inevitably undermine effective partnership working in this area.

The development of judicial protocols
The Public Law Outline

The Public Law Outline (PLO) (MOJ, 2008) introduced in England and Wales in April 2008 initially appeared to hold out the promise of a fairer process for parents. Whilst the rhetoric of the PLO to provide an alternative form of dispute resolution outside of the court may at first reading appear less adversarial and therefore proportionate to the issue being considered, there are tensions and dilemmas in relation to ensuring that the rights of parents and children are protected when important decisions are being made without the oversight of the court. Despite the rhetoric of keeping children and families at the heart, there appears no relief from the procedural and managerial processes set within a context of public sector cuts affecting all professionals tasked with protecting children. Achieving justice for children and families to ensure their rights are protected within a protocol that necessitates increased resources remains a challenge.

As part of an ongoing review of policy and practice in safeguarding children in the UK, and as a response to the inquiries into child deaths or serious case reviews in the 1990s and post-2000, a number of important policy and legislative changes have been introduced. These changes are intended to optimize outcomes for children and families by reducing delay in the conduct and resolution of cases, and by ensuring that costs and resources are effectively managed at all stages of a child protection case. This book is concerned not merely with achieving diversionary approaches with respect to children either 'on the edge of care', or within public law proceedings, as for some children the local authority should be making an application to court. The reader is invited to consider the implications of a move towards making a greater number of highly consequential decisions in complex child protection cases within administrative rather than judicial settings, either within public law or private law proceedings, and to ensure child protection practice pre-proceedings focuses on detailed assessments and planning for children and their families.

It is my contention that recent developments in policy and practice have introduced yet further instrumental approaches to child protection that undermine the potential to engage effectively with parents (Broadhurst and Holt, 2010). In setting the arguments with the aim of stimulating debate, I am prompted by reflections of the constructions of children and their parents and the perceived potential of many parents, if offered appropriate support, to care safely for their children (Holt and Kelly, 2014b).

The aspirations to reduce delay within the family justice system

The aspirations of the Public Law Outline are well rehearsed and detailed (Broadhurst and Holt, 2010). Thus it is important to state that it set in train significant changes to child protection practice by introducing a deadline of 26 weeks for the completion of the majority of care cases with the enactment of the Children and Families Act in April 2014. The Family Justice Review (MOJ, 2011a, 2011b) and revisions to the Public Law Outline included in the Practice

Direction 36C – Pilot Scheme: Care and Supervision Proceedings and Other Proceedings Under Part 4 of the Children Act 1989 (MOJ, 2013) support the overriding objective to ensure proportionate use of resources within the timeframe for the child.

Furthermore, the Public Law Outline replaced the Protocol for Judicial Case Management (MOJ, 2003) in England and Wales and required a reordering of the way care proceedings are instigated, structured and conducted. The PLO involves two stages: 'pre-proceedings' and 'post-instigation of proceedings'. In the latter, the court process is reduced from six to four stages, each with explicit timescales attached to procedures, and the local authority is required to provide a detailed core assessment and care plan at the 'issuing of proceedings and first appointment' hearing.

In the pre-proceedings stage the aim is to maximize the possibility of resolving cases without proceedings and make mandatory certain steps that are to be taken prior to proceedings being issued. These require the local authority to: carry out assessment work prior to the instigation of proceedings; identify and assess any possible alternative placements with relatives and friends; and explore all possible alternatives to instigating proceedings. Should the local authority consider that proceedings are necessary (and not of such a nature that the welfare of the child requires immediate court protection) they must convene a meeting between the social worker and local authority legal advisor (a legal planning meeting), and a 'letter before proceedings' must be sent to parents. This letter must summarize concerns, state actions required to remedy those concerns, provide information on what the local authority has done to safeguard the child to date and state what outcome would be likely if the concerns are not addressed. The letter before proceedings invites parents to 'a pre-proceedings meeting' to be convened with the local authority legal advisor and social worker/s, and must advise parents on how to obtain legal advice and representation at that meeting.

Whilst these procedures may have been in place in local authorities prior to the PLO, the mandatory nature of the pre-proceedings stage means that parents now have a more formal statement of their position and clear information that they have the right to legal representation at the pre-proceedings meeting. These changes place further emphasis and demands on local authorities to seek and evidence mediated alternatives to local authority care and continue to be underscored by the 'no order' principle of the Children Act 1989 (Welbourne, 2008).

The Public Law Outline (MOJ, 2008) outlined a new approach to care proceedings by formalizing and making certain activities mandatory at the pre-proceedings stage. Furthermore, it specified timescales, should cases proceed to court (Broadhurst and Holt, 2010; Masson et al., 2013). This document provided a checklist of what should be completed at the pre-proceedings stage. This included: carrying out all relevant assessments; issuing a 'letter before proceedings' to parents outlining the requirement to attend a pre-proceedings meeting (PPM); and holding a PPM where the local authority specify concerns and what parents must do if they are to keep their children. The outcome of that meeting is an 'agreement' with the parents of the changes required of them and the timescales within which they must be demonstrated.

The timescales associated with stages in proceedings were as follows. At stage 1, issue and first application should occur by day 6; at stage 2 a case management conference should be held no later than day 45 and a timetable for the child will be set; at stage 3 an issues resolution hearing should occur between 16 and 25 weeks; and at stage 4, the final hearing and resolution should take place according to the timetable for the child (but should be by week 26).

In section 3.14 of the PLO 2008 (pp.4–5) it stated that the court must actively manage cases and this included reference to encouraging and facilitating parties to use an alternative dispute resolution procedure if appropriate and in the interests of the child to do so (section 3.14). A further section (section 18, p.18) elaborates on alternative dispute resolution emphasizing that, where appropriate, parties can ask the court for advice about alternative dispute resolution and if the court considers it appropriate, proceedings may be adjourned for periods of time to facilitate such an approach.

In the amended PLO (Practice Direction 36c, 2013) timescales are revised and reference to alternative dispute resolution has been removed. In stage 1, issue and allocation, day one should see the local authority attaching specified documents to the application, and day two should see the local authority serving on the other parties the 'checklist' documents. The filing and service of documents is to be considerably more focused than previously and wherever possible restricted to the last two years. Stage 2, the case management hearing, should take place by day 12 (and if a further case management conference is to be held this must be no later than day 20). Stage 3, the issues resolution hearing, should take place in accordance with the timetable for the proceedings, which should be within 26 weeks. In effect this practice direction explicitly locates alternative dispute resolution and working with parents in pre-proceedings work (Broadhurst et al., 2013).

A refocusing on dealing with cases in a more robust manner before an application to court is crucial to achieving swift case resolution when the court is required to intervene in a family matter. Hence, the front-loading of all assessment work was built into the PLO with a clear mandate for pre-proceedings work. Moreover, this is supported and reinforced by the Practice Direction 36c, the revised Public Law Outline 2014 and the Children and Families Act 2014, which reinforced the emphasis on working with parents and undertaking assessments of families in administrative pre-court work. As the deadline for the resolution of cases following an application to court is 26 weeks, this leaves little time for parents to turn their lives around once an application to court has been made (Holt et al., 2013a).

Increasing flexibility to work within the formal pre-proceedings stage where parents have been put on notice of the local authority's intention to issue care proceedings may be an appropriate, and last, place to try to engage in partnership working, but there are two pertinent issues. First, effective pre-proceedings work may result in case resolution in 26 weeks should the case progress into proceedings; but it may simply result in delay being introduced at an earlier stage without judicial oversight and scrutiny (Holt *et al.*, 2013). Second, two important studies by Broadhurst *et al.* (2013) and Masson *et al.* (2013) have examined the formal pre-proceedings space. Significantly, within these studies accounts from both parents and professionals highlight considerable national variability in the availability of resources and the quality of pre-proceedings practice.

Alongside the erosion of the intent and opportunity to engage with parents, it is argued that this supports the work of Featherstone, Broadhurst and Holt (2012) which shows that policy and practice changes have led to an increased emphasis on instrumental and tightly defined approaches to parents (in practice, mothers). Further, that such instrumental approaches that emphasize procedure, assessments and conditional requirements by parents if children are to remain in their care potentially makes decision making an activity where sight of the social and holistic context of families' needs may be lost. Conditional requirements of parents that carry strong temporal imperatives have exacerbated already existing difficulties in terms of local authorities developing meaningful partnerships with them (Featherstone *et al.*, 2010). This may also be particularly problematic when there are child protection concerns and where the likelihood of court action has been proposed as a strong possibility, resulting in the potential for partnerships to become adversarial (Broadhurst *et al.*, 2012).

Furthermore, it is suggested that an under-explored issue has been, at worst, hostility and at best, ambivalence, to seeing parents (particularly mothers) as worthy of concern in their own right rather than simply as conduits for ensuring the welfare of their children (Featherstone *et al.*, 2010). In such a climate it is not surprising that social workers consider 'putting your children first' is absolutely at the heart of what parents, in all sorts of circumstances, and operating under a variety of constraints, should do. It is thus assumed that if parents put their children first it is axiomatic that they will cooperate with the local authority – even if in practice they are not at all clear why they should, or what such cooperation might entail (Kaganas, 2010).

Administrative decision making and the rights of parents and children to be consulted

The absence of any system for bringing local authorities to account for the failure to adhere to care plans has been a concern amongst members of the judiciary for the last 15 years. The initial decision of the Court of Appeal in *Re W and B; Re W (Care Plan)* [2001] was met with approval. Two innovations were fashioned by the Court of Appeal. First, the court enunciated guidelines intended to give trial judges a wider discretion to make an interim care order, rather than a final care order. The second innovation was more radical. It concerns the position after the court has made a care order. The Court of Appeal propounded a new procedure, by which at the trial the essential milestones of a care plan would be identified and elevated to a 'starred status'. If a starred milestone was not achieved within a reasonable time after the date set at trial, the local authority were obliged to 'reactivate the interdisciplinary process that contributed to the creation of the care plan'. At the very minimum the local authority was required to inform the child's guardian of the position. Either the guardian or the local authority would then have the right to apply to the court for further directions. However, this position was not supported when the government responded to the overturning of that decision by the House of Lords in *Re S (Minors) (Care Order: Implementation of Care Plan); Re W (Minors) (Care Order: Adequacy of Care Plan)* [2002] by introducing the legal requirement for an independent reviewing officer (IRO) to be appointed for each looked-after child. The Court of Appeal decision (now referred to as *Re S and Re W*) was perceived as the court appointing itself as the monitor of the local authority and its responsibilities towards children in their care. The House of Lords confirmed that it was not for the court to take on that role; legislation was needed to create a formal monitoring of the duties held by the local authority.

An amendment to section 26 of the Children Act 1989 (made by the Adoption and Children Act 2002) created a statutory duty to appoint an independent reviewing officer to participate in case reviews, to monitor the local authority's performance in reviews and to consider whether it would be appropriate to refer cases to the Children and Family Court Advisory and Support Service (Cafcass).

The role of Cafcass to prioritize the interests of children involved in family proceedings, by undertaking detailed assessments to advise the court on what they consider to be in the best interests of children, is stretched with a move to proportionate working practices. This has resulted in less time for the important face-to-face work that underpins good decision making (Holt *et al.*, 2014).

It is undoubtedly the case that there are children, whether protected children or children in need, whose human rights have been breached by the actions (or inactions) of local authorities (Jay, 2015). In a climate where resources are overstretched and politics increasingly influence practice decisions, there has never been a time when independent scrutiny by another professional is so important. There is a political drive to move increasingly towards resolving disputes in an administrative space, namely the local authority; and yet there is little evidence that dispute resolution processes in many authorities have been used historically or, indeed, that such processes even exist in some authorities. Where administrative decision making occurs without the oversight of the court, the problem of not involving or hearing children may be compounded by the fact that care plans may have no effective independent scrutiny (*S v Rochdale* [2008]). This case illustrates that although procedures do exist to ensure independent and effective review, these sometimes fail. Article 8 (ECHR) therefore applies equally to administrative decision making in exactly the same way as decisions made within court proceedings (*Re B (Care: Interference with Family Life)* [2003]). In child protection cases, Article 8 guarantees fairness in the decision-making process, and the procedural safeguards mandated by Article 8 should apply equally to decisions that are made at the pre-proceedings stage.

There are inevitably cases where administrative decision making by a local authority has been challenged within the judiciary. For example, the European Court of Human Rights on 16 March 2010 in *AD and OD v United Kingdom* ruled that failure by a local authority to conduct a risk assessment, resulting in a child being placed with foster parents, was a breach of Article 8.

Furthermore, where family members become involved in the care of a child within pre-proceedings protocols, there have been examples of local authorities negotiating an arbitrary fee that falls below the rate usually offered to foster carers (Holt *et al.*, 2013a). This issue was raised in *R (L and Others) v Manchester City Council* [2001], where Manchester City Council's policy on payments to kinship carers was successfully challenged as a result of the local authority adopting a policy of paying less to relative foster carers. This effectively prevented the continuation of a family placement and as a result the rights of the child under Article 8 were not respected. The action was taken against the local authority as a result of the decision made at the pre-proceedings stage to pay short-term kinship carers of looked-after children significantly less than approved local authority foster carers. However, once approved as long-term carers by the local authority they were paid at the normal rate.

Munby J found the local authority policy to be both irrational and contrary to Article 8 of the ECHR. The impact of the judgment is that payments to kinship carers must be made on the same basis as local authority carers whether it is a short-term or long-term arrangement. Any difference should relate to the child's needs, the skills of the carer, or some other relevant factor that is used as a basis for an authority-wide policy.

Discussion

It is now accepted beyond doubt that both parents and children are persons under the Convention and that children too possess 'Convention rights'. As well as parents, the child is afforded exactly the same procedural guarantees, protection and fairness mandated by Article 8 (*Re S* [2004]). That children have a right to be heard is further highlighted in *W v W* [2010] and *Re D (Abduction: Rights of Custody)* [2006].

Baroness Hale of Richmond commented:

> They [children] are quite capable of being moral actors in their own rights. Just as the adults may have to do what the court decides whether they like it or not, so does the child. But that is no more a reason for failing to hear what the child has to say than it is for refusing to hear the parents' views. *(Re D (Abduction: Rights of Custody)* [2006] UKHL S1 [S7])

Child care law is peppered with similar cases that highlight the requirement to hear what the child has to say. The recent high-profile child sexual exploitation cases, notably in Rotherham and Oxfordshire, but not exclusively in these authorities, show the failure of local authorities to listen to and respond to the voice of the child, as is highlighted in the Jay report (Jay, 2015).

Whilst child care law remains dominated by the concept that the child's welfare is paramount (*Re KD (A Minor) (Ward: Termination of Access)* [1988]), there is a tension between the paramount principle and the Convention in practice. Significantly, the focus on the child's welfare tends to divert attention away from the child's rights (Featherstone *et al.*, 2010). Consistently evidenced in child death inquiry reports and serious case reviews, the child's right to participate meaningfully in the decision-making process, and right to be heard, are often not afforded its due significance (Brandon *et al.*, 2009).

In child protection practice it can be seen that the ECHR requires the state to engage in a most sensitive balancing exercise. The incorporation of the Convention has implications for the way in which local authorities conduct themselves in performing their statutory role, and for the allocation of their resources.

CHAPTER 2

The Remote Control Approach in the Family Courts

A Dickensian Misadventure?

Introduction

The changes to legal aid introduced with the implementation of the Legal Aid, Sentencing and Punishment of Offenders Act (LASPO) 2012 has resulted in an unprecedented number of claimants who are unrepresented in the most complex of cases, following relationship breakdown and where negotiations and agreements need to be achieved in respect of children. There have been scenes of violence in the courtroom and, consequently, additional litigation. Ironically this has resulted in increased costs rather than achieving the reduction anticipated by the introduction of new legislation that is premised on achieving dispute resolution by an alternative means within a pre-proceedings protocol, rather than proceeding to court. However, it appears that the policy of the Ministry of Justice to reduce the legal aid bill may have been counter-productive, but the implications for families who turn to a system when they are most in need, and for front-line professionals working with the most complex families, are far-reaching (Family Group Unions Parliamentary Group, 2014).

The Judicial Executive Board, whose members comprise the most senior judges in England and Wales, submitted a response to the Justice Committee Inquiry: Civil Aid on 13 May 2014. Tasked with examining the changes introduced by LASPO, it highlighted significant concern in respect of a system that is in crisis (MOJ, 2014a).

A significant impact of changes in response to cuts in legal aid has been the increased security required in courts. The evidence submitted to the committee highlights the substantial problems of litigants in person arriving at the court, often with friends and family in train to offer advice and support in the absence of legal representation. Scenes resembling a Dickensian novel are evident in the courtroom, where Pickwick was attempting to deliver his papers without any knowledge or understanding of the rules of court etiquette. Whilst this Dickensian image may hold a literary appeal, set within a 21st-century family justice system that is premised on the rule of law and achieving fair, just and proportionate remedies, the appeal falls short (Holt, 2013).

Tensions are reported to be high between rival parties in the waiting areas, which prior to the introduction of LASPO would have been brokered more effectively by legal advocates who were skilled in navigating this difficult and emotive terrain. Instead, these tensions have to be managed by court ushers, other party representatives, pro bono representatives, the local authority social worker, if involved with the family, and members of the judiciary. Inevitably there have been reports of incidents of violence that on occasions have been significant – presenting a significant risk to court staff and members of the public in the waiting area (Bar Council, 2014b).

Furthermore, there has been a significant increase in the number of cases where one or both parties arrive at court without legal representation, and this is most commonly observed in private law family matters. In these cases, legal aid has been removed and individuals are required to represent themselves unless they can afford to pay for legal representation. The impact on court efficiency has been hugely significant. Whilst the government may have achieved the intended savings to the legal aid budget, the changes introduced with LASPO have resulted in spillage elsewhere in the system. The unintended consequences – although I may have a different view about this assertion, given the dominant political discourse around welfare – is the absence of legal representation for some of the most complex families. This has resulted in parents having to defend themselves against both the local authority, who will employ the most experienced of family and child care lawyers and experts, and other parties, usually men, who can afford legal representation. Several reported cases highlight the injustice for all, but for women and parents with complex needs in particular (*Re H* [2014], which is discussed more fully below).

The courts, in particular the county courts, are simply not equipped to deal with unrepresented litigants who arrive with the aim of resolving a legal dispute in complex family matters without the required knowledge or understanding of court etiquette and with no professional advocate to advise and to attempt to arrive at a settlement outside the court. Prior to the introduction of LASPO a great deal of time and skill was employed in attempting to reach an amicable settlement between the parties immediately prior to the court hearing, which afforded the opportunity for parties and their advocates to have separate rooms, with legal advocates moving between rooms to negotiate with their professional colleagues on behalf of each party. In practice this allowed a degree of protection, as legal advocates would attempt to broker an effective outcome for their client, ensuring the welfare and protection of children were considered. The result of these negotiations was presented to the judge, who would consider the agreement before making a judgment in the case and a final order (Holt, 2013).

The prospect of resolving cases that may have previously avoided the court having to hear the case in full is limited. Parties are now arriving at the hearing without legal representation and are being required to outline their case in full to the judge. Clearly, there are territory skirmishes with tensions high and alternative versions of the facts being shared in front of the other party and the judge. If tensions are not dissipated prior to the parties entering the courtroom, the potential for a further escalation of violence is high. A substantial number of private law hearings are conducted by district judges in chambers that are compact and without access to the same level of space and security as a courtroom. Relevant parties, the judge and clerk are sitting in close proximity within the courtroom. Without the knowledge and understanding of court etiquette, it was entirely foreseeable that in such a highly charged environment with so much at stake, there have been outbreaks of anger with parties engaged in violence during the hearing (Byron, 2014).

The system of advocacy has a long tradition within the English legal system (Holt, 2013). Advocates are experts, with extensive training in negotiation and conferencing skills, and are therefore able to navigate proficiently the difficult terrain of complex family matters with individuals who, if they were able to resolve matters amicably, would have done so before arriving at court. Relationships are therefore highly charged, in anticipation of a hearing whereby there is so much at stake. The prospect of achieving effective brokering at an earlier stage to avert a fully contested hearing, when individuals are under so much stress and without legal representation, is limited (Broadhurst *et al.*, 2013).

The role of legally trained and professional advocates is to attempt to resolve matters at an earlier stage to avoid the additional stress of highly personal details being shared in court, which is likely to prompt further contestation. It is exactly these scenes that are now being enacted within courtrooms throughout England and Wales, with litigants in person requiring more judicial involvement as they attempt to manage their own fully contested hearing, including the cross-examination of estranged parties with whom they are locked in a dispute (Holt, 2013).

The result of these changes is widespread chaos in the family court with anecdotal accounts of parties shouting and screaming at each other; the judge attempting to keep control; security being elicited to restrain individuals who are being escorted out of the courtroom to enable them to calm down; and, in some instances, hearings being adjourned to a later date as the parties are too distressed to progress. The impact on delays across the civil, family and tribunal justice systems cannot be underestimated, and the resulting spillage elsewhere in the system is inevitable when families turn to the local authority to assist when they are in such crisis (Byron, 2014).

The introduction of LASPO was intended to result in a shift away from cases progressing to court. In reality, the number of cases resolved by mediation has fallen, as there has not been the anticipated take-up of this service, resulting in more cases progressing to the courts and tribunals (Holt, 2013).

In addition to the problems associated with litigants in person, the removal of funding for expert reports in private law family cases has compounded the crisis in the family courts. The lack of pre-proceedings advice in the most complex of cases may have resulted in an increase in unmeritorious claims and, without question, some meritorious cases never being brought (Bar Council, 2014a).

Changes to legal aid

Whilst the cost of legal aid in the UK has indeed been one of the highest in the world at around two billion pounds annually, the removal of legal aid has unintended consequences for the claimant, the professional advocate and the public (Holt and Kelly, 2015d).

The recent cuts to the legal aid scheme reflect a dominant discourse that is less tolerant of welfare and the recipients of welfare. However, the attack on legal aid has denied help to more than 400,000 people a year; in reality this means more than 1000 people every day are denied access to justice. There are 5000 people a month involved in cases that go to court who previously would have obtained legal representation, but under the new rules are unable to do so. It is therefore not surprising that we are now experiencing far more litigants in person in the family courts and reported cases of injustice and unfairness in terms of outcomes for children and their families, as evidenced in the cases referred to later in this chapter (Byron, 2013).

The intention and effect of LASPO was to radically reduce the availability of legal aid across family and civil cases. Of the 400,000 people denied legal aid by the Act, 160,000 were married couples involved in family disputes. Nearly 230,000 were individuals confronted by housing, employment and social welfare problems. In the first nine months since the introduction of LASPO over 50,400 parents, almost six out of ten cases involving family cases relating to children, had no legal representation (MOJ, 2014a).

The availability of legal aid was a significant issue in *Re H* [2014]. HHJ Hallam challenged the injustice of the changes to legal aid following a case whereby a mother who had complex health needs, including impaired vision and hearing and who was deemed to have significant learning disabilities, was required to represent herself at court in respect of a custody hearing in relation to her children. HHJ Hallam stated the following in relation to a clear breach of Articles 6 and 8 of the ECHR:

> In the absence of legal aid to secure representation of the mother, it is inevitable that her article 6 and her article 8 ECHR rights will be at risk of being violated, given her evident speech, hearing and learning difficulties, if the case proceeds without further representation. I cannot see how anyone can come to the conclusion that this mother's article 6 rights were not in jeopardy. The father has the support of a legal representative, the local authority, who are advancing a case contrary to that of the mother's, has legal representation. Without legal aid, therefore, the mother, on her own, would be facing two advocates pursuing a case against her, on any basis that cannot be equality of arms. She is the party with the least ability, the greatest vulnerability, and she should have had the benefit of legal representation. In effect, this vulnerable mother is faced with two advocates running a case against her and she does not even have one. I cannot think of a clearer breach of article 6. Article 8 – this matter is clearly about family life and the mother's

right to family life, whether the children should be in her care or not and what contact she should have. (*Re H* [2014] EWFC B127)

Furthermore, Sir James Munby, President of the Family Division, has joined in the condemnation of the cuts to legal aid for the most vulnerable parents who are left to defend themselves when decisions are being made in respect of their children. In an unprecedented move in *Q v Q; Re B (A Child); Re C (A Child)* [2014], Justice Munby delivered a judgment that provided a direct challenge to the government over the policy regarding legal aid, and warned the Ministry of Justice in this case that costs would have to be met by Her Majesty's Courts & Tribunals Service if a father's right to a fair trial were to be upheld.

Moreover, in *Re D (A Child)* [2014], where the matter related to the removal of a child from parents with significant learning difficulties by Swindon Borough Council, Justice Munby gave the following judgment:

> What I have to grapple with is the profoundly disturbing fact that the parents do not qualify for legal aid, but lack the financial resources to pay for legal representation in circumstances where, to speak plainly, it is unthinkable that they should have to face the local authority's application without proper representation. (*Re D (A Child)* [2014] EWFC 39 [3])

The reality of losing a child without being able to represent themselves owing to their own difficulties, is clearly a breach of their rights under Articles 6 and 8, ECHR. Justice Munby cited the more recent decision of the Strasbourg court in *RP and Others v United Kingdom (Application No 38245/08)* [2013].

He further highlighted the chaos in respect of legal aid and the fundamental challenge to the rule of law when he stated:

> The state has simply washed its hands of the problem, leaving the solution to the problem which the state has itself created – for the state has brought the proceedings but declined all responsibility for ensuring that the parents are able to participate effectively in the proceedings it has brought – to the goodwill, the charity, of the

legal profession. This is, it might be thought, both unprincipled and unconscionable. Why should the state leave it to private individuals to ensure that the state is not in breach of [its] obligations under the convention? (*Re D (A Child)* [2014] EWFC 39 [3])

Ensuring parents receive fair access to justice in the most complex of cases due to the reforms of fees and the reduction of experienced solicitors undertaking family work was initially raised by Judith Masson when she examined in considerable detail the implications of controlling costs whilst maintaining services in the important area of family work. The issues the family justice system are experiencing now were fully anticipated in 2008 (Masson, 2008).

Furthermore, Masson suggested then that a two-tier system was very likely to emerge, resulting in a local authority having a distinct advantage in terms of access to the most experienced legal advice and representation, and parents in contrast finding it difficult to find an experienced representative. In respect of *Re D* above, Justice Munby provides evidence that Masson's concerns have come to fruition when a parent was faced with defending herself against the local authority with no legal representation. The implications of LASPO and the Legal Services Commission Fee Scheme Guidance (2011) have resulted in unequal access to legal representation and impacts on parents' ability to comply with section 11 of the Children and Families Act 2014 that presumes parental involvement.

In *Re K-H (Children)* [2015], the question of the rights of children was highlighted in a case that has raised considerable concern amongst members of the judiciary and lawyers representing children. The appeal was brought by the Lord Chancellor against the decision of His Honour Judge Bellamy sitting as Deputy High Court Judge in *Re K and H (Children: Unrepresented Father: Cross-Examination of child)* [2015].

The matter concerned a request by the father to have contact with his children, namely, K and H. The mother's eldest daughter, Y, made allegations that she was sexually abused by the father. In order for the court to determine the truth of the allegations and what impact, if any, there would be to K and H, there was to be a fact-finding hearing. The court determined that Y would need to give live evidence to the court and as the father could not afford legal representation, he would be required to cross-examine Y. His Honour Judge Bellamy made the decision that the cost should be met by Her Majesty's Courts & Tribunals Service (HMCTS) to allow a qualified advocate to cross-examine Y on behalf of the father. The case raised so much concern with both the Association of Lawyers for Children and Coram Children's Legal Centre that they applied to the Court of Appeal to intervene, and permission was granted. The Court of Appeal upheld the appeal of the Lord Chancellor and so found that the judge's decision was wrong and that there was no power for the judge to order HMCTS to provide the funding.

The government's solution

In response to the unprecedented number of litigants in person and the concerns raised by the Judicial Executive Board, the government's solution, initiated by Simon Hughes, Family Justice Minister in the previous coalition government, was to provide a network of in-court advice centres throughout England and Wales. These will provide support for litigants in person in civil and family matters that will be funded by the Ministry of Justice. The initiative aims to provide assistance to claimants who are not entitled to legal aid to navigate the complex legal terrain in the areas of law that involve family disputes, clinical negligence, welfare benefits, employment, housing, debt, immigration and education. These are fundamental issues that impact most significantly on those individuals who are in need of welfare support as a result of experiencing multiple vulnerabilities (MOJ, 2014a).

The aspirations of the changes introduced with LASPO may have been well intentioned. However, the introduction of a system requiring individuals to seek alternative forms of dispute resolution prior to an application to court being made – thereby reducing the number of cases that progress to court and the resources available to support litigants – is simply not working. Whilst it can be argued that the state should not be required to intervene and inherit the financial burden of private family matters, the reality is that these cases often involve children experiencing vulnerabilities and adults who have complex needs. Providing appropriate support is likely to be more challenging in the family courts where parties who are in dispute may require urgent assistance to resolve matters where children are involved.

The current situation is proving to be untenable, with members of the judiciary being required to intervene throughout the hearing to ensure all the parties understand the legal process. This is resulting in increased time, resources and costs, the very issues the government sought to reduce. The family courts are described as being at breaking point (Byron, 2014).

The Personal Support Unit, with an estimated operational cost of £1.14 million per annum, has been introduced to provide advice within the court centres in England and Wales. The remit of the unit is to provide advice to claimants and to make links between claimants and pro bono lawyers who are able to offer free legal support and, in some instances, court representation. Advisors will not necessarily be qualified lawyers; they may include law graduates, students undertaking law training and retired individuals with professional backgrounds (MOJ, 2014b).

Mitigating the worse effects of the cuts to legal aid with a reduced package of support may well be a political ploy to allay a perceived widespread condemnation of these changes, but it does not address the need for claimants and it does absolutely nothing to retain good advocates who are working in these important areas of law. There is a pressing need to attract and retain good advocates particularly at a time when austerity cuts are having considerable impact on the most vulnerable within our society (Holt *et al.*, 2013a).

Whilst the Personal Support Unit may be relatively inexpensive to operate, it is potentially problematic when this service is being operated by a range of individuals with varying degrees of skill and knowledge of the legal processes. It appears to be a service that is a formalized version of the McKenzie friend, presumably with few of the problems attached, except perhaps current knowledge of the law, as they will at least be impartial in the case. Advisors will have no right of audience in court but may be permitted to sit next to the claimant in court for support.

Furthermore, universities are encouraging law students to engage in clinical legal education in the form of law clinics and advice centres that provide students with legal experience under supervision. Whilst this may indeed improve the skills of the student, there are obvious dilemmas in so far as students may excel in their legal studies, but due to the changes introduced by LASPO may never be in a position to elicit paid work in the areas in which they are developing skills (Torsney and Henderson, 2013). There is a strong possibility that we will encourage law graduates away from publicly funded work, as this will be almost non-existent, and encourage graduates to prioritize possessions over people and move into the more lucrative areas of law. In the meantime, we must not lose sight of the impact on the claimant who is at the mercy of whoever is willing to offer advice regardless of their knowledge and skill in this area.

The aim of the reform is clearly to move claimants away from the court and to encourage, through a telephone and online advice service, alternative forms of dispute resolution outside of the court in the form of mediation and the Children and Family Court Advisory and Support Service (Cafcass). The implications for Cafcass cannot be underestimated, and it is placing yet further pressure on a service that is already overstretched and employing proportionate working practices in an attempt to cover the work (Holt *et al.*, 2014).

The impact of cuts to legal aid – a further attack on welfare

> We currently deal with around 500 welfare benefits cases a year including large numbers of appeals across the whole range of welfare benefits…our clients are typically vulnerable for a number of reasons, for example physical and mental health problems, chaotic lifestyles, poor literacy and language skills, severe poverty and living in poor quality and insecure accommodation. (Torsney and Henderson, 2013, p.22)

The study also highlighted children as being at particular risk, for whom the withdrawal of legal aid for private family law might mean losing contact with a parent. 'Advice deserts' are likely to expand rapidly, leaving the most vulnerable without legal assistance. Legal firms that have historically relied heavily on legal aid work have closed, resulting, in some areas, without any legal firms remaining even if individuals had the financial means to obtain help. Experienced lawyers with considerable knowledge and skills, who were highlighted by the Family Justice Review in 2011 as a strength of the Family Justice System, have gone. An unprecedented number of legal professionals have either lost their jobs and/or switched areas of law, or have made a decision not to enter this area of law, in favour of a career that will elicit financial security. It is an extremely worrying situation for the future of family law and in the absence of an urgent rethink it is difficult to see how the situation can easily be reversed.

There is a disparity between the policy documentation depicting the kind of society the government espouses with the reality of an austerity climate for those who are most in need and professionals who are tasked with providing help to challenge the injustices. The continued preoccupation with achieving targets and reducing costs ignores the complexities of individuals and families who seek welfare support (Jordan and Drakeford, 2012).

Academics and senior members of the judiciary are challenging a culture of compliance with rules that are aimed at the most vulnerable (Featherstone *et al.*, 2014; *Re D* (see earlier)). Judgments from senior members of the judiciary in the form that we have seen in this chapter are a significant development that places the judiciary and the administration in direct conflict. It is evident that the current Conservative government continues to adopt the same repertoire – namely a focus on remote control measures that are designed to reduce costs that impact most significantly on individuals and families who are reliant upon welfare and who often experience multiple vulnerabilities (*Re K-H* earlier).

The impact of changes to legal aid will have both intended and unintended consequences for claimants and members of the legal profession. Achieving case resolution swiftly and justly must be at the heart of a family justice system that purports to hold children and their families as a priority when they are most in need and at times of crisis. Parents will have less time and resources to retrieve their position within the court arena. Proposed changes introduced with LASPO and the Children and Families Act 2014 indicate a less tolerant approach to welfare and to parents who seek state support (Grover, 2008).

In this context, effective advocacy for parents is critical to ensuring that outcomes for children and their parents are fair, equitable and proportionate (Holt, 2013). In a climate of austerity that has seen a sustained attack on welfare, and the recipients of welfare more specifically, ensuring that parents are subject to fair decision-making processes at all stages in the process has never been so urgent or necessary (Featherstone *et al.*, 2011).

The role of good professional advocacy and legal advice, given the increasingly regulated and highly instrumental procedures that are employed within public services, is crucial, as this may be the only opportunity available in which to broker an effective remedy on behalf of parents, and to facilitate alternative solutions. In practice, the erosion of funding for legal advice over the last two decades, and the resulting loss of experienced legal professionals, have contributed to the quality and availability of legal representation for parents that is at best 'patchy' (Freeman and Hunt, 1998; Lindley, 1994; Masson, 2012).

Case study

Let us consider the case of Bertie, Kelly and Hassan in Chapter 1. If Hassan initiates divorce proceedings, and let us make the assumption that he can afford legal representation, where would this leave Kelly in terms of legal representation, particularly if the local authority were to intervene in the proceedings to determine where Bertie should live?

Alternatively, the local authority may decide to hold a pre-proceedings meeting due to concerns regarding the likelihood of Bertie suffering significant harm. Who will advocate on behalf of Kelly, Hassan and Bertie at the meeting? What potential issues should be considered and what challenges may be presented, particularly if the family live in an area which is an advice desert where no legal firms specializing in family law remain (see Chapter 3)?

Discussion

In a climate of austerity for all claimants and professionals involved in the family justice system, installing what Newman *et al.* (2008) describe as *transactional processes* that focus on the regulation of standards with a government steer that produces compliance is persuasive.

However, the changes introduced with the Legal Aid Sentencing and Punishment of Offenders Act 2012 have resulted in the most vulnerable individuals and families being left unsupported when they are most in need. In particular, this book has highlighted several cases whereby parents are not merely unrepresented, but face having to present their own case when the local authority and other parties have legal representation. This situation is clearly unacceptable, but what is more disturbing is a society that, in the first place, allows this position to arise. The injustices that we are currently witnessing were indeed foreseeable; legislation has been enacted with the clear intention of individual parties paying for private litigation that has been previously funded by the state. However, the state in some circumstances initiates the action, and an individual has no choice but to respond, as we have seen in the cases of *Re H* and *Re B*, which both involve complex family matters that require a decision to be made about where a child should reside. It is evident that there needs to be a rethink of current policy and legislation, as the solutions the government has proposed thus far are not adequate to address the injustice that many families are now experiencing in the family courts.

Moreover, with an increased concern with the timescales and costs and a less tolerant approach to welfare, the changes being introduced with the cuts to legal aid are being absorbed into a climate of compliance and control. Rather than engaging in relationship building, discretion and professional judgement, advocates and members of the judiciary are increasingly navigating tensions on the front line – this in itself highlights a move away from the richness of relationships and the promotion of families' rights, and replacement with a culture driven by procedure and regulations (Holt and Kelly, 2012b).

There is an urgent and pressing need for all professionals working within the family justice system to challenge the impact of both economic and social poverty and its complex links with knowledge, power and access to justice (Castell, 2007). Challenging the injustice for families in this context is crucial if we are to reverse the trend for a less tolerant approach to welfare, and to retain the principles of the rule of law and natural justice that underpin the English legal system (Neuberger, 2013).

CHAPTER 3

Mediation

The Holy Grail of Reforms to Working with Complex Families

Introduction

Following the implementation of both the Legal Aid Sentencing and Punishment of Offenders Act (LASPO) 2012, and the Children and Families Act 2014, mediation has been heralded by the government as the holy grail of reforms by effectively diverting cases away from court by a range of alternative forms of dispute resolution.

The Family Procedure (Amendment No 3) Rules 2014 (SI 2014/843) and the FPR 2010 Practice Direction 3A – Non-Court Dispute Resolution provide the statutes and statutory instruments that require the court to consider at every stage in the proceedings. This includes whether a non-court dispute resolution is appropriate and if a Mediation Information and Assessment Meeting (MIAM) took place, or whether an exemption was confirmed and if the parties attempted either mediation or another form of non-court dispute resolution, and the outcome. The court has the power to adjourn proceedings if it considers non-court dispute resolution is appropriate. It is worthy of note that the term 'non-court dispute resolution' has replaced the previous term of 'alternative dispute resolution'; whilst fundamentally the aspirations of both are for parties to reach agreement or consensus on the important issues, namely financial, property and arrangements in relation to children following the breakdown of a relationship, the non-court dispute resolution quite explicitly requires parties to engage in non-court resolution regardless of whether they chose to do so.

However, adopting non-court dispute resolution approaches to resolving matters, in particular mediation, is not a novel idea. In Europe, where mediation is used as a form of dispute resolution in divorce proceedings, it is clear that it is not 'one size fits all' and at best it is described as patchy:

> A picture of mediation in Europe would resemble a constantly changing patchwork quilt or mosaic. The pieces making up this patchwork have recurring patterns and colours, but they are not uniform and they are not woven to a single design. There are many missing pieces and the patchwork has gaps in it. A variegated patchwork that recognises cultural differences is preferable to uniformity. (Parkinson, 2005, p.9)

In the UK there has been a shift towards non-court dispute resolution both within private law and public law proceedings, with the term 'mediation' used within private law disputes and the pre-proceedings protocol within public law proceedings. The aspirations of the government in relation to both are to ensure within a structured protocol that parties reach an agreement at an early stage, wherever it is safe and possible to do so, to avoid the need for the matter to be dealt with in court, and thereby saving time and cost. The state nevertheless remains in control, but remotely; the protocol is highly procedural and regulated and the state can chose whether and at what stage to intervene.

The rhetoric of attempting to reach an agreement between the parties without the need for a court hearing that will inevitably introduce a degree of adversarial contestation is difficult to dispute. When individuals are facing enormous turmoil in their personal lives they should be able to resolve these matters without their personal information being shared in court, where historically the system is highly bureaucratic and impersonal (Holt and Kelly, 2014a).

Private law

Despite the intentions of the legislators and policy makers there are occasions when, in private law disputes, mediation is neither an appropriate nor an effective remedy. This may be because of the power imbalances within the relationship, and/or where there has been any form of abuse between the parties, where disputes over the placement of children cannot be agreed, or where capacity issues are relevant.

Since the introduction of mediation in private law matters, there continues to be relatively low take-up by parties, arguably for the reasons stated above – the matters involved are often highly complex and require the skill, experience, impartiality and knowledge of a judge to resolve. Despite the lack of appetite for mediation the government continue to progress on this course with further incentives to entice parties to enter mediation prior to making an application to court. The term 'mediation' is confusing for parties as it implies an attempt at reconciliation, and only if this is not successful then a settlement out of court should be sought – this interpretation continues to be a feature within Europe, where take-up of mediation continues to be low (Stanić, 2005).

In order to attempt to keep the government's agenda on course the Ministry of Justice announced on 3 November 2014 that in the event that one party has legal funding, the government would fund both parties' attendance at one appointment for mediation. Given the *without prejudice* nature of mediation, there are a limited number of reported cases that highlight both the court's powers to persuade parties into mediation, and the consequences for parties who unreasonably sabotage, for example by refusing to attend (Holt and Kelly, 2015c).

There exists a fundamental confusion between mediation and reconciliation. Whilst they are indeed separate tasks, with reconciliation focused on, say, attempting to save a relationship and mediation principally aimed at achieving an amicable separation, the perceptions of parties is that they are one and the same, and this view

men, deliberately chose mediation as a vehicle to control their partners in the process.

> The effects of legal aid changes in the Legal Aid, Sentencing and Punishment of Offenders Act 2012 (LASPO) have put added pressure on practitioners to be inclusive rather than exclude borderline violent and coercive control cases, where self-representation at court is seen as a worse fate for such vulnerable parties. Better screening, safer systems and effective triage for all cases are needed, alongside supported alternatives, to avoid the risk of agreements that always favour the 'stronger' party. (2014, p.8)

Significantly, only 26 out of 61 parties resolved their children's disputes by means of ADR (43%), whereas in respect of financial matters the position was more positive with 51 out of 76 parties able to resolve their financial disputes by means of FDR (67%).

The three-year project found that individuals who were more reluctant to engage with mediation tended to be more dissatisfied and reported that it was less effective. The project also highlighted the ability of one of the parties to determine the choice of non-court dispute resolution. This would effectively block available options to the other party, hence exposing how the rhetoric of the voluntary nature of ADR can be seen as providing choice, but the reality on the ground is quite different, especially for the party with less power in the relationship.

The landscape post-LASPO is that many parties have the choice of either legally aided mediation or self-representation in court. The rhetoric introduced with both the LASPO and the Children and Families Act 2014 is that alternative forms of dispute resolution are the best option, and making an application to court is the worst option. However, as the recent study by Barlow *et al.* (2014) has highlighted, where complex issues exist, such as resolving disputes relating to children, alternative forms of dispute resolution are not always appropriate. Where parties have experienced violence or intimidation, the prospect of mediation can be traumatic.

Whilst every attempt should be made to resolve matters without the need to go to court, it needs to be acknowledged that in some instances going to court earlier may indeed be the most appropriate course of action. Particularly where individuals, usually women, hold less power, the gravitas of the court can provide a place to negotiate and broker more effective resolutions where there are complex issues at stake.

Case study

We refer again to the case study in Chapter 1.

Kelly has spoken to her social worker to express concern that she has continued to experience domestic abuse throughout the marriage and is frightened of Hassan.

Kelly disputes the allegations that she is using alcohol and drugs and is concerned that she will lose Bertie because of her past history and the real possibility that Hassan will be able to put forward a much stronger case. What advice/support can you provide to Kelly?

Public law

In public law proceedings the possibility of resolving disputes when the state has interfered in family life is even more difficult. In these situations parents face the prospect of losing a child, and from the position of the parent, the local authority holds the power. Following the implementation of the Public Law Outline in 2008, parents are issued with a 'letter before proceedings' to inform them that the local authority intends to make an application to court owing to concerns about the welfare of their child. In a recent study by Holt *et al.* (2014), *Liverpool Pre-Proceedings Pilot Final Report*, it was found that in the majority of cases where the local authority had initiated the pre-proceedings protocol, the family were already known. The average time that a child was known, from the point of referral to the local authority making an application to court, was three-and-a-half years. Clearly, any attempt to resolve matters to avoid an escalation to care proceedings had been attempted at a much earlier stage, prior to the local authority sending the parents a letter outlining their concerns and inviting them with their legal representatives to a pre-proceedings meeting. Mediation in this context is therefore a highly contested approach to resolving complex family situations which require the oversight, experience and independence of the court (Holt and Kelly, 2015c).

There is a somewhat intractable tension within the law and policy between normative concerns with parental autonomy (hence the impetus to achieve safe diversion to avoid the need to go to court) and a children's rights perspective. This is evident in the recent rhetoric of the 'timetable for the child', which has been introduced to justify a deadline for the completion of cases within 26 weeks following an application to court, but makes no regard for delay introduced elsewhere in the process (Luckock, 2008).

Nowhere are these tensions more apparent than in the context of child protection, where the state, as discussed, can impose clear limitations on parental autonomy (Corby, Miller and Young, 1996). Working with parents in this context can make achieving agreement outside of the courtroom hard to achieve – note that in care proceedings, the failure of parents to cooperate is frequently cited as a key precipitating factor for the local authority initiating care proceedings (Brophy, 2006).

It is a concern that to require an enforced period of pre-proceedings work, when the family may have already been known to the local authority for a lengthy period of time, is merely shifting delay to a different space. The child could be left holding the risk for a longer period without the independent oversight of the court, especially in situations where there are complex issues that involve the most vulnerable families who are turning to a system when they are most in need and in crisis. Moreover, given the competing policy and resource imperatives as discussed, the implementation of the Revised Public Law Outline 2014 and the Children and Families Act 2014 may not yield the outcomes that are intended.

Interestingly, the problem is that when any new administrative process is introduced, such as alternative forms of dispute resolution, questions and energies are then directed at examining whether these new processes are operating effectively. This is a somewhat inevitable consequence of the self-referential nature of legislation and policy making, but it leaves other, perhaps more fruitful lines of enquiry outside of the frame. My contention is that the important issue relating to delay is that the digitization of social work management has removed social work resources away from front-line practice to a target-driven service that is risk averse with a culture of error and blame. A lack of case management within the judiciary has allowed the social work assessment to be replaced with a plethora of expert reports that often provide nothing additional but safety in numbers. The rise of the Ofsted inspection regime has resulted in an overly bureaucratic cut-and-paste system of recording that departs from the rich narratives of practice. This culture is dispiriting and demoralizing for professionals, who are operating within a climate of error and blame. The introduction of yet further procedures and protocols will do nothing to change this but will undoubtedly add to the burden for professionals who will view it as having to jump through yet more hoops, and creating unfairness for children and their families, who will also be required to navigate this difficult terrain with little prospect of a swift solution (Holt, 2014a).

Front-line practitioners – namely lawyers and social workers operating within the family justice system who have the responsibility for working with individuals who experience the most vulnerabilities – have seen increasing amounts of their time for engaging in this work eroded owing to severe cuts to public spending and legal funding. Successive government policies have impacted on the recruitment and retention within both professions, and over the last decade the most experienced have left the professions, with the resulting loss of organizational memory, skill, knowledge and experience.

Moreover, professionals operate in an increasingly regulated and restricted climate, characterized by the standardization of both assessment and response (pre-birth assessments, parenting assessments, timescales, formats, 26 weeks and so forth). This is coupled with a less tolerant and more punitive approach to welfare (Grover, 2008).

The practical and psychological pressure for professionals and parents to trade an agreement at the pre-proceedings stage for the promise of escaping judicial criticism can prove irresistible, particularly following the judgment handed down in *Re B-S (Children)* [2013], which provides a sharp reminder to all professionals who appear at the courtroom that despite attempts to jump through all the hoops, criticism is never far away.

In a country that has withdrawn legal aid for the majority of family work, the costs of defending yourself against the state that is seeking to remove your children could cost you everything. The need for experienced professionals to advise and support children and their families during times of crisis and when they are most urgently in need has never been so crucial. In some instances, professionals have undertaken this important work for free (see *Re D (A Child)* [2014] in Chapter 2).

The crisis in the family justice system reflects a dominant discourse around welfare that is less tolerant and plainly punitive (Jordan and Drakeford, 2012). Legislation such as the LASPO Act 2012 and the Children and Families Act 2014 have been introduced with the intention of reducing the financial burden of welfare on the state. The message is abundantly clear: families who experience difficulty must only turn to the courts or state as a last rather than first resort, unless they have the financial resources and thereby the social and economic power to navigate the system (Holt, 2014a). In reality, families who are experiencing stress and are reliant upon welfare support will be required to turn to the local authority and other agencies to assist them – the court is only one arm of the state. The savings in this area will undoubtedly be met by other publicly funded organizations who are already overstretched and under-resourced.

Importantly, the child and the family appear to have become lost in a family justice system that has become preoccupied with funding and timescales.

In *Re D (A Child) (No 2)* [2015], the President returned to the funding issues that first gave him much concern in *Re D (No 1)* [2014]. The final hearing in this matter was approaching but legal aid had not yet been confirmed for the final hearing. The President stated that he would:

> view with the very gravest concern any suggestion that they should be denied legal aid on 'merits' grounds. Given the extreme gravity of the issues at stake and their various problems and difficulties, it is, as I said before (*Re D*, paras 3, 31), unthinkable that the parents should have to face the local authority's application without proper representation… This is a case about three human beings. It is a case which raises the most profound issues for each of these three people. The outcome will affect each of them for the rest of their lives. Even those of us who spend our lives in the family courts can have but a dim awareness of the agony these parents must be going through as they wait, and wait, and wait, and wait, to learn whether or not their child is to be returned to them. Yet for much of the time since their son was taken from them – for far too much of that time – the focus of the proceedings has had to be on the issue of funding, which has indeed been the primary focus of the last three hearings. The parents can be forgiven for thinking that they are trapped in a system which is neither compassionate nor even humane. (Tughan, 2015)

The legislative changes introduced following LASPO and the Children and Families Act 2014, and recent decisions from the Supreme Court and Court of Appeal, should serve as a reminder as to how the state gains and rarely gives up power over individuals, and the relative ease with which significant changes are introduced without question or challenge. These changes then become permanent features over time that are rehearsed and reinforced (Holt and Kelly, 2015d).

Furthermore, it is important to note that human rights are universal, and a right to a fair trial when the state intervenes in family life should be central in a democratic society, and protection under the law should not be dependent upon an accident of birth or economic power. Legislative changes that have been introduced with little resistance can be seen as a direct attack on welfare, and are counter-productive in terms of achieving justice for children and their families. There has been mounting concern regarding the cost of welfare on the state, but the scenes observed in courtrooms nationally portray a shameful picture of a society that purports to hold the welfare of the child as the paramount consideration, whilst simultaneously employing a Draconian approach to resolving disputes for some children whose parents are powerless to defend themselves when the state intervenes to remove their children. This is a result of a removal of the right to legal representation in the majority of private law disputes, and a deadline for the conclusion of proceedings in public law (Holt and Kelly, 2015d).

Case study

Kelly, following an incident where it is alleged that Hassan has been violent towards Kelly, calls the police. On arrival at the home the police recognize Hassan, who is known to them in relation to a number of prostitutes who claim to work for him. The police also confirm that Kelly has worked as a prostitute whilst married to Hassan, but they don't have any evidence to suggest that she is currently working.

The police arrest Hassan, and the social worker visits Kelly, who appears low in mood, frightened and unwilling to talk about her relationship with Hassan or to provide any information in respect of her early childhood.

The local authority is concerned for Bertie's safety, although he is currently making good progress developmentally and appears to have a good attachment to Kelly. The social worker advises Kelly that a child protection conference will be held, together with a pre-proceedings meeting, and delivers to Kelly a letter before proceedings, outlining the concerns of the local authority and inviting both Kelly and Hassan to a meeting with the local authority to which they are advised to seek legal advice.

Given the current situation what advice/support needs to be given to Kelly and Hassan and what form should the meeting take?

There has been no assessment of the family. What assessments are needed to determine the risk to Bertie and who should undertake these?

Discussion

Throughout the last decade the dominant discourse around welfare, but more specifically the recipients of welfare, has unashamedly reflected a less tolerant approach, with tabloid headlines that seek to blame individuals who experience a range of vulnerabilities (Jordan and Drakeford, 2012).

Equality before the law and access to justice are fundamental pillars of our democracy. Legal aid was introduced over 65 years ago by the post-war welfare reforms to facilitate access to justice for all. During the last two decades successive governments have eroded the legal aid budget by a series of measures, notably reducing the financial eligibility criteria and creating 'advice deserts', where there are no legal aid solicitors providing advice in a category(s) of law in particular geographical areas, resulting in many individuals being unable to access affordable legal help. The introduction of the Legal Aid, Sentencing and Punishment of Offenders Act 2012 that came into force in April 2013, with limited exceptions, removed legal aid for family law, clinical negligence, welfare, employment, immigration, housing, debt and education. Framed by the government as the reform of the family justice system, in reality the Act has been described by commentators as a '*bloodbath*' for legal aid and justice for individuals who are most in need and who turn to a system at times of crisis (Tweedale, 2015).

The government have purported to a strong commitment to protect legal aid for victims of domestic violence who are seeking to leave violent relationships. The entitlement to legal aid to help individuals leave abusive relationships has been a failure, as the regulations, both in terms of evidence requirements and income or asset thresholds requiring financial contribution, have resulted in a significant number of individuals abandoning their rights to justice (Baksi *et al.*, 2014).

Significantly, it is women who are faced with the prospect of navigating this difficult and complex terrain when they are in crisis and the choice is not straightforward, particularly when the risk for women at the point of leaving is heightened. The availability of legal help is pivotal to ensuring women and children are able to leave violent relationships safely and to secure arrangements for children, housing and finance following the separation to ensure that women and children are protected (Office for National Statistics, 2013).

Whilst the rhetoric of attempting to resolve matters, whether in private law or public law matters in a manner that is less adversarial in nature, is admirable and difficult to dispute, the landscape is not quite so straightforward. If the choice is removed and individuals are forced into reaching agreements by alternative forms of dispute resolution that remove the oversight of the court, there is a real potential for injustice and risk. It could lead to some individuals making the decision to remain in a violent relationship which may place themselves and their children at risk, rather than face taking legal action without legal help. Where arrangements are made out of court, for example, through mediation, that are either unjust or unworkable, this may result in a propensity for litigation at a later stage when these arrangements break down.

I am not persuaded by the rhetoric that the reforms have been essentially driven by the timetable for the child. In reality, within public law proceedings children are waiting just as long for disputes to be resolved and arguably longer (Holt *et al.*, 2013a) whilst parties and professionals navigate the pre-court terrain. In private law, the abolition of legal help could leave women and children where there is domestic violence at increased risk of harm, and potentially children could remain in situations where they are experiencing violence for much longer periods (Baksi *et al.*, 2014).

These challenges are indeed global, and therefore must be viewed in an international context, with an adherence to the principles that underpin the Human Rights Act 1998 and the rights established within the European Convention on Human Rights, to ensure that individuals are protected (Chakrabati, 2014).

Whilst there is a desire to avoid an adversarial resolution of complex disputes located within a context of emotional distress and conflict for the parties, this requires appropriate resources that do not appear forthcoming in a climate of austerity and cost-cutting (Treloar and Boyd, 2014).

Regardless of the context, innovations such as mediation and other out-of-court forms of dispute resolution require adequate resources to ensure these services can be delivered by professionals who are working to resolve disputes and for parties to reach agreement, within the most complex situations and when individuals are often in a highly emotional state. There will be situations where alternative forms of dispute resolution are not appropriate, and making an application to court is the most appropriate course of action. The court must never be seen as the last resort; in some circumstances involvement of the court at an earlier stage in the process may be pivotal in terms of reaching an early decision and thus avoiding delay for children and their families. Decisions that are made following the breakdown of a family are life-changing and there is a need for the most experienced of social work and legal professionals to be involved in this process.

Whilst the rhetoric of reforms to the family justice system that emphasize the importance of achieving consensual solutions within the context of child protection may be well intentioned, the challenge remains for all professionals involved in the process to ensure that parents and children are sufficiently represented when important decisions are being made without the oversight of the court. This is particularly vital in a context of extensive public sector cuts, a move to proportionate working practices amongst key professionals and defined court timescales, which will allow no opportunity for repeat assessments once a case has progressed to court.

CHAPTER 4

Why Parents Matter

Exploring the Impact of Instrumental Approaches to Resolving Complex Situations

Introduction

The remote control approach to working with children and their families is highlighted in an increased emphasis in the last decade on approaches to working with parents that are highly instrumental, procedural and regulated and which serve to heighten already strained relationships between parents (usually mothers) and the local authority. Achieving good partnership working within this context is difficult and, particularly where there are child protection concerns and the tangible threat of court proceedings, all forms of contact become adversarial (Featherstone *et al.*, 2010).

Approaches to parenting have become increasingly instrumental from the point of initial contact. From initial assessments, core assessments, parenting assessments, child protection plans, pre-proceedings protocols, court proceedings and permanancy planning, each stage has an allocated timeframe that prompts the next stage. The social worker remotely controls each stage from the safety of the computer – tasked with populating progress – which is viewed remotely by line managers to judge whether there has been compliance with the requirements. There is no room for slippage; off-the-shelf packages of care are provided and there is an expectation that take-up yields results within weeks, otherwise there is an escalation to the next stage of the process. These approaches fail to recognize the potential of parents, if offered appropriate support and relationship-based approaches to practice, to care safely for their children (Dumbrill, 2006). The impact of austerity measures in the context of the now-hegemonic concern with the timetable for the child have further contributed to a strained relationship between the local authority and parents (Featherstone, Morris and White, 2013).

It is absolutely imperative and legitimate that decision making for children is undertaken in a timely manner, as the consequences for children when delay and poor planning are introduced is significant (Luckock and Broadhust, 2013). My concern is when the timetable for the child is used to support a modernization agenda (MOJ and DfE, 2012) which is principally aimed at reducing costs when a case goes to court. This indeed supports timely decision making, but lacks the flexibility to respond to less instrumental approaches (Holt and Kelly, 2012a).

The Family Justice Review (MOJ, 2011a) established a direction of travel for the resolution of both public law and private law cases that is not readily reversible (Broadhurst et al., 2013). The modernization agenda, as we have discussed in the previous chapters, is shifting the burden of resolving the most complex of cases to the administrative space of pre-court social work, mediation or another form of dispute resolution that does not involve the court. Whilst the aspirations of the government to reduce court costs may yet be achieved with a shift in emphasis to front-loading the work to an earlier stage, let us make no mistake – the costs will similarly shift to the local authority and the delay for children will simply move to an earlier stage without judicial oversight and scrutiny (Holt et al., 2013a).

Furthermore, two important studies by Broadhurst et al. (2013) and Masson et al. (2013) have examined the formal pre-proceedings space. Significantly, within these studies accounts from both parents and professionals highlight considerable variability in the availability of resources and the quality of pre-proceedings practice. In response to the findings from both studies, with the modernization agenda of the family courts (MOJ and DfE, 2012) and the focus on the timetable for the child, it is imperative that we explore ways to ensure that parents and their children remain central to the family justice system (Featherstone *et al.*, 2010).

These important issues resonate with broader national and international debates that seek a review of a child protection and family justice system that is viewed as highly procedural and intimidating by parents. Moreover, where the rights of parents to be afforded the opportunity to demonstrate their potential by engaging in relationship-based interactions with professionals who are tasked with forming a judgement about their capacity, capability and competence as parents is denied (Ferguson, 2004).

The rhetoric and reality of achieving partnerships with parents within a policy context of remote control practice

The challenge for practitioners is how to establish and maintain partnership working when the organizational priorities are focused on gathering information within a highly procedural context, leaving little time for relationship-based work, which is the essence of social work practice (Parton, 2014a).

Partnership working is a collage of rights, duties and recommendations grounded in laudable but abstract terms, only some of which are grounded in practice, but all of which are interpreted 'on the ground'. For example, a great deal of use is made of terms such as 'partnership', 'cooperation' and 'consultation'. These terms are vague and 'leave considerable room for interpretation and that can mean different things in different situations' (Kaganas, 1995, p.4). The notion of partnership working is both implicit and explicit in a

focuses on strengths could ultimately alter her status (Swain, 2009). In the context of achieving a holistic assessment of the family it could also significantly improve the outcome for Bertie and Kelly – which could be life-changing.

Although the government response to the Family Justice Review (MOJ and DfE, 2012) places parents and children at the heart of the process, on close examination of the impact of both LASPO and the Children and Families Act 2014, the focus appears to be on cutting costs and standardizing out-of-court disputes within both private and public law proceedings and severely curtailing court timescales when a matter does proceed to court (Holt, Broadhurst, Doherty and Kelly, 2013a). The timetable for the child conveniently supports the aspirations of the policy makers to reduce delay for children, and is consistent with the principles of the Children Act 1989, but the rhetoric does not appear to be supported with any additional resources for local authorities who are already buckling under the strain of increased regulation and inspection and with severe resource constraints, despite the recommendations of the Munro report. In summary, there appears to be no relief for a profession that is highly regulated and bureaucratic, and the consequence of not complying is to apportion individual error and blame (Holt *et al.*, 2013a). A culture of compliance with rules and regulations has replaced the practice of social workers relying upon professional judgement and discretion (Jordan and Drakeford, 2012).

Furthermore, as the Children and Families Act 2014 has cemented the family justice reforms to reduce the length of care proceedings to 26 weeks for public law proceedings and to remove the right to legal aid in the majority of private law proceedings (MOJ and DfE, 2012), the work undertaken with parents in either out-of-court dispute options for private law matters or within pre-proceedings meetings for public law matters will be essential, because parents will have less time to retrieve their position within the court arena (Holt *et al.*, 2013a).

Changes that have been implemented with the LASPO and the Children and Families Act 2014 reflect a clear shift away from reassessment of parents during court proceedings, with the aim to reduce delay in the family court, emphasizing the hegemonic concern with the timetable for the child coupled with a less tolerant approach to welfare and waiting for parents to change (Grover, 2008).

In this context, effective advocacy for parents within pre-proceedings will be critical to facilitate engagement with the issues that are being raised by either parent, another party or the local authority. Despite the concerns raised in Chapters 2 and 3 in respect of the changes to legal aid and the impact of some parents being unable to access legal help owing to either a lack of finance or advice deserts in some areas of the UK, it is inevitable that the local authority (together with a range of pro bono agencies and advice centres) will be more heavily relied upon to navigate this difficult terrain to ensure parents have the opportunity to maximize opportunities for rehabilitation and to ensure the rights of parents and their children are protected (Holt *et al.*, 2013a).

The role of professional advocacy/legal advice within increasingly regulated and highly instrumental procedures has never been so pivotal in terms of being able to broker a good deal on behalf of parents and to facilitate alternative solutions. However, in practice the evidence highlights that both the quality and availability of legal representation for parents are at best patchy, and at the most extreme, not available (see *Re D* earlier).

Pre-proceedings processes are now formal within both private law and public law proceedings. These are distinct in so far as they seek to fuse welfare concerns with the threat of legal proceedings if disputes cannot be resolved and a way forward that secures the child's situation cannot be agreed. Parental perceptions of the pre-proceedings meeting is of a highly regulated and procedural protocol. It provides further opportunity for the local authority to gather evidence within public law proceedings (Holt *et al.*, 2013a), or to support a parent within private law proceedings, whereby the parent who isn't supported is left without legal help, facing both the other party and the local authority who are legally represented (*Re D* earlier).

Discussion

The changes that have been introduced following the Family Justice Review (MOJ, 2011a), the Legal Aid Sentencing and Punishment of Offenders Act 2012, Children and Families Act 2014 and a raft of judgments from the Supreme Court and Court of Appeal (which we will examine in Chapter 6) have been revolutionary. The abolition of legal aid (introduced over 60 years ago for family work) and the move to a single family court (tasked with reducing delay and improving efficiency by front-loading cases to either a pre-proceedings protocol or a non-court dispute resolution – Mediation, Information and Assessment Meeting (MIAM)) have irreversibly transformed family work in two years.

With all this in mind, we now turn to addressing concerns that are central to ensuring that parents are afforded the advice, support, information and guidance they need at the earliest opportunity. It is clear that the quality of all pre-proceedings assessments, including the social work assessment, will need to be holistic in nature and to explore the possibilities for safe and effective diversion of cases that are on the edge of care. Importantly, issues of representation for both children and their parents during this pre-proceedings stage are crucial to ensure rights are protected within a climate of austerity. All professionals working with families during the pre-proceedings stage will need to reflect upon the dominant discourse around welfare, to ensure resources and services reflect need and are deployed justly and equitably, with a recognition that working within highly regulated and bureaucratic systems can result in the development of a risk-averse culture that introduces instrumental approaches to working with parents that rely on a remote control, rather than a relationship-based, approach to social work practice (Holt and Kelly, 2012b).

It is understandable that social workers operating under pressure and within an audit-and-blame culture may avoid collective solidarity (Jordan and Drakeford, 2012). A colleague who had the misfortune to sit through one of my lectures and who is neither a social work nor a legal academic rose to her feet, much to the bemusement of trainee social workers and lawyers alike, and said 'Why are we all sitting here? It is outrageous – we should be marching from somewhere to somewhere...' The reality on the ground is somewhat different. Lawyers are leaving the profession in droves, either due to redundancy or not choosing to take family law as a specialism in the first place, so there are few left to march anywhere. In terms of social work, as a profession that has recently seen the closure of the College of Social Work with little challenge from either politicians or practitioners, we need to question where the voice is of a profession that is tasked to work with the most vulnerable individuals and communities.

Members of the judiciary, legal profession and social work profession must be careful not to sacrifice justice before the altar of reducing costs and resources (Welbourne, 2014). Professionals working within the family justice system need to acknowledge the impact of both social and economic poverty and their significance in relation to knowledge, power and access to justice (Castell, 2007).

CHAPTER 5

Decision Making and Planning for Children

The Need for a Holistic Assessment of the Family and an Understanding of Permanency Planning

Introduction

Assessing risk and making decisions in complex situations requires not only the individual attributes of skill and judgement, but also support and resources from both the individual agency and the courts. There are consequences that flow from every decision that is made in respect of a child where there are child protection concerns – these are life-changing (Holt, 2014a).

In Chapter 4 there was a focus on the importance of working in partnership with parents within the family justice system to ensure effective decisions are made in respect of their children. Whilst working with parents is unquestionably important, it is fundamental that the welfare of the child must always remain the paramount consideration for all professionals regardless of their role within the family justice system. The child's welfare, not costs, resources or timescales, must remain the focus.

The legislative changes that have been introduced during the last two years have indeed eroded the rights of some parents to justice, and the spillage from these changes will undoubtedly be required to be supported elsewhere in the system. However, we need to be aware that within this context it could be easy to focus on the needs and competing agendas of the adults within the family, whose needs may be complex, and to make assumptions from assessments of the parents about the needs, wishes and feelings of the child. It is imperative that assumptions about the child are not made, and that resources are given to spending time with children to ensure they are fully listened to and included in the assessment. Furthermore, social work practitioners tasked with representing children must be able to address the questions raised in the welfare checklist, section 1(4) of the Children Act 89, and consider whether they have detailed knowledge of the child sufficient to be able to address the checklist and identify the needs, wishes and feelings of the child. Effective communication and engagement with children, as well as ensuring they have a voice and are heard within meetings that are largely adult focused, is crucial in child protection work (Lefevre, 2010).

Despite the plethora of legislation, guidance and case law, evidence suggests that the child largely remains silent in child protection procedures, and regardless of the reform of the family justice system, delay and planning for children remain unacceptable. There may have been a reduction in the case duration once an application to court has been made, but there is clear evidence of drift, with some children waiting up to three years for a decision to be made about their future; however, this is hidden away from public scrutiny within a pre-proceedings protocol (Broadhurst, Holt and Doherty, 2011; Holt *et al.*, 2013a).

In response to the concern regarding the visibility of children within the pre-proceedings stage, Broadhurst and colleagues fashioned the innovation of introducing the family court advisor within the pre-proceedings meetings to ensure the voice of the child was central to both the meeting and the decision making (Holt *et al.*, 2013a). It is clearly evident from this study that the inclusion of an advocate for the child at these important meetings was successful in keeping the focus on the child, but it highlighted the concern that without this degree of independence it is all too easy for professionals to focus on the competing needs and agendas of the adults.

Changes introduced with the revised Public Law Outline 2014 and the Children and Families Act 2014 mandated a deadline of 26 weeks for the completion of the majority of cases that proceed to court; these, coupled with changes introduced with the Legal Aid Sentencing and Punishment of Offenders Act 2012 (LASPO) that came into force in 2013, have reduced access to judicial scrutiny of complex cases, with a focus on out-of-court settlements. We must be clear that a reduction in court time does not equate to a reduction in delay for children – the delay has shifted to a much earlier stage in the process. Social workers are already navigating the territory skirmishes of highly regulated and bureaucratic practices, and with the introduction of the 26-week deadline, the family justice system is operating like a pressure cooker with children building up underneath; either they are waiting for a crisis to occur that will lift the lid and propel the case to court, or they remain under the radar for longer periods whilst professionals are focused on the next crisis that has to be dealt with. Professionals are measured in terms of whether or not they are compliant with the deadline set by the court, for which there are clear consequences. In a climate of error and blame it is easy to see why professionals remain compliant to the court; and this compliance is reinforced by the judgments that are handed down, particularly from the Supreme Court and Court of Appeal, but also the lower courts who have the power to enforce adherence to the rules (Holt, 2014a).

Given the deadline for the completion of the majority of cases within 26 weeks, it is crucial that good assessment and planning takes place at the earliest opportunity and all the options for the child are fully explored. In the process of weighing up all the options available for the child, there needs to be an analysis of risk in arriving at a care plan for the child. This message was reinforced by the Supreme Court decision in *Re B (A Child) (Care Proceedings: Threshold Criteria)* [2013] in June 2013, followed by the Court of Appeal in *Re B-S (Children)* [2013], who delivered a judgment on 17 September 2013.

Judgments from the Supreme Court and Court of Appeal: implications for practice

The judgment delivered by Mr Justice Holman in *A and B v Rotherham Metropolitan Borough Council* [2014] on 5 December 2014 has put into effect the changes that were set in train by *Re B (A Child) (Care Proceedings: Threshold Criteria)* [2013] and *Re B-S (Children)* [2013].

Before considering the facts in *Re A and B*, it is perhaps important to consider two landmark cases that were initially thought to have paved the way for an increase in parental challenge to placement and adoption orders; however, in practice there is clear evidence that whilst parents may challenge placement and adoption orders, the state rarely gives up power, and leave to appeal will still feature only in a minority of cases.

The Supreme Court decision in *Re B (A Child) (Care Proceedings: Threshold Criteria)* [2013] in June 2013 created the landscape for a number of significant judgments that have raised concerns about the current practice in relation to permanency planning for children (notably: *Re V (Children)* [2013]; *Re S, K v The London Borough of Brent* [2013]; *Re P (A Child)* [2013]; and *Re G (A Child)* [2013]).

Furthermore, it has been suggested that it was the unanimous judgment of the Court of Appeal in *Re B-S (Children)* [2013] that has paved the way to 'calling a halt' (paragraph 30) to current practice, which was considered to be not good enough, in terms of permanency planning for children.

Following the judgments in *Re B* and *Re B-S* it was inevitable that we would see an increase in the number of applications by parents contesting the making of an adoption order, as these cases exposed a weakness in local authority decision making and planning in respect of children and, if they therefore had the grounds to do so, parents could challenge the local authority. However, it must be stated that leave to appeal a placement order must be based on cogent reasons, as the implications for parents, potential adopters and children are significant.

The Court of Appeal provides clear guidance to be taken in cases where the plan for the child is adoption, and has restated the test for the granting of leave to oppose an adoption order contained in section 47(5) of the Adoption and Children Act 2002. In granting leave to oppose an adoption order the court has to be satisfied that there has been a change of circumstances. If there is evidence of a change in circumstances of a nature and degree, there is judicial discretion to grant leave, but in making this decision the judge has to be guided by section 1, Adoption and Children Act 2002 that the paramount consideration of the court must be the child's welfare throughout his or her life (*Re P (Adoption: Leave Provisions)* [2007]).

The facts of *Re B-S* are both well rehearsed and reported, but it may be helpful to briefly outline the details here. The children in this case were placed for adoption in April 2012 and the mother applied for leave to oppose the adoption orders in 2013. The Court of Appeal, on hearing this matter, took the opportunity to reinforce the key points from the recent Supreme Court decision in *Re B* [2013]. In brief, the child's interests are paramount, and those interests include living with the birth family. Furthermore, the court must consider all the *realistic* available options, and in assessing the birth family's capacity to care for a child, judges must consider the support the family could be offered (Luckock, 2008).

The President in *Re B-S* clearly stated that, although he couldn't say that for some children adoption is not the right option, he asserted that adoption must be the last rather than first resort, and crucially, the decision to place a child for adoption must be taken following a detailed analysis of all the realistic options available, and this should take place at the earliest opportunity (Doughty, 2013).

In the event of a local authority considering removing a child from the birth family, the message from both the Supreme Court and Court of Appeal is very clear. It is imperative that before such a move takes place, and ideally within the pre-proceedings stage, there is a need for a deep analysis of all the realistic options available, and wherever possible and safe to do so the local authority should attempt to keep the child in the care of the birth family before a placement order is made. The court is under a duty to consider the welfare of the child throughout his or her life, and the local authority should have the same in mind when making decisions around permanency. In this respect, the decision in *Re B-S* has significant and wide-ranging implications for adoption practice in England and Wales.

Case study

Let us refer back to the case study of Kelly, Hassan and Bertie. At the point where the local authority are considering issuing a letter before proceedings, there needs to be a weighing-up of all the pros and cons of each realistic option for Bertie. The process of weighing up all the options will continue throughout the pre-proceedings stage, whereby it may be necessary to undertake detailed assessments with extended family members. For example, in order to reach a reasoned and informed recommendation should rehabilitation with parents not be an option, and in the event that no agreement can be reached in terms of placement with extended family members, an application to court will need to be made to place Bertie either with extended family members or outside of the family. The Court of Appeal advises professionals and members of the judiciary to use a balance-sheet-style analysis, which may be helpful in weighing up the pros and cons of each option.

Following the decision in *Re B-S* it was widely anticipated that there would be a reverse trend in local authorities seeking both placement and adoption orders, and this would introduce further delay for children who may have longer to wait before a final decision on their future is made. Indeed, local authorities are heavily persuaded and influenced by judgments from the court, but even more so from the Supreme Court and Court of Appeal. Social work is a profession that is regularly portrayed by the media in negative terms, which feeds into workers' perceptions of their value and judgements. Social workers fear scrutiny and challenge by the court, which was initially evidenced in a reduction in the number of placement and adoption orders applied for, but this position is not sustainable – the decision to apply for a placement or adoption order must be made with confidence following a detailed and informed assessment of the family (Holt, 2014a).

Whilst the court should expect evidence of the highest quality in the most complex cases, the reality of social work practice on the ground is one of confusion and uncertainty following recent judgments in respect of permanency planning for children. The case of *Re A and B v Rotherham Metropolitan Borough Council* [2014] is distinct on the facts and probably unique, but nevertheless it has ignited the debate amongst social work and legal professionals in respect of whether challenge from birth parents when an adoption order is applied for should be permitted.

Whilst this case divided professional opinion following the judgment, I am not persuaded by the argument that it will have a significant impact on the decision of a local authority as to whether to make an application for a placement or adoption order. However, the case may have implications for the recruitment of adopters who may be unwilling to enter a potentially uncertain legal landscape, and if realized, this is likely to have profound implications for children.

Re A and B v Rotherham Metropolitan Borough Council [2014] EWFC 47

It may be helpful to provide some brief details here, although this case is reported and the judgment is well worth a read. The case concerns a child aged 20 months who was placed with adopters at the age of even months and who has lived with the adopters for 13 months. The child's mother had significant problems related to alcohol and drugs, and the child was removed from the mother and accommodated with foster carers shortly after his birth. The mother identified her then partner as the child's father, and all the professionals involved accepted this despite the fact that the child had dark skin compared with his parents. The mother's partner asserted that his mother was of Burmese heritage and this was accepted. The care plan of adoption and the placement order were unopposed and the placement order was granted. The child was placed with potential adopters and it wasn't until the adopters applied for an adoption order that the issue of parentage became evident. The child's father, who was not the mother's partner at the time the child was removed, came forward and following DNA screening parentage was confirmed. The father was not seeking to care for the child directly, but suggested to the court that the child should be cared for by his sister, the child's paternal aunt, to enable him to grow up within his birth family.

Whilst the mother of the child and the prospective adopters were white, the father and his sister were black African. The case divided professional opinion: the social workers and psychologist involved with the family were in support of an adoption order being made; the director of safeguarding children and families, the interim strategic director of children's services and the child's guardian were firmly opposed to the making of an adoption order, despite the fact that the child had settled well and there was evidence of a good attachment with the adopters.

An independent social work assessment in respect of the aunt was positive and there was a clear commitment to work with social workers, should the decision be made to place the child in her care.

The aunt had a child of her own who had been made aware of the prospect of another child joining the family. Mr Justice Holman was clear that he was not adopting the test of whether nothing else would do, but rather made the decision on the basis of the child's welfare throughout his life:

> If the balance of factors came down against making an adoption order it would not be made. If the issues were evenly balanced and it was not possible to say that making an adoption order would be better for him than not doing so then an adoption order would not be made. (*Re A and B v Rotherham Metropolitan Borough Council* [2014] EWFC 47 [15])

Mr Justice Holman made the decision that it was positively better for the child not to be adopted but to move to live with the aunt. The adoption application was dismissed and pursuant to section 24(4) of the Adoption and Children Act 2002, the placement order would be revoked.

The facts in this case are unprecedented and the case will undoubtedly attract strong opinions on either side. Regardless of whether there is a meaningful legal right to challenge an adoption order at this late stage (judgment of Lord Justice Munby in *Re J and S (Children)* [2014]), the consequences for the recruitment and retention of adopters is significant.

Mr Justice Holman explained his decision in respect of the timing of the application to oppose the making of an adoption order by the child's father:

> It is accepted by all concerned in this case that if the father had come forward and the true paternity had been established at any time up to the moment when the child was actually placed with A and B, then he would not have been placed with them and, after due assessment of her, would almost certainly have been placed with the aunt. (*Re A and B v Rotherham Metropolitan Borough Council* [2014] EWFC 47 [5])

Whilst this may have been the outcome if either of the parents had notified the local authority of the child's true parentage at an earlier stage, to be allowed to challenge the making of an adoption order when the child has been living with the prospective adopters for 13 months departs from the recent judgments in *Re C (A Child)* [2013] and *Re J and S (Children)* [2014].

The President in *Re C* reaffirmed the principle that a judge who properly applies section 1 of the 2002 Act will normally be compliant with the requirements of Article 8 and in this respect (and in connection with Article 6) highlighted the case of *YC v United Kingdom (Application No 4547/10)* [2012].

The President considered the potential appeal against the adoption order made on 2 April 2012. It was accepted that the father had the right to appeal against the order, even though he was not a party to the proceedings at the time it was made. The President confirmed that the law sets a very high bar against any challenge to an adoption order and once lawfully and properly made can be set aside only in 'highly exceptional and very particular circumstances'.

Furthermore, the President stated in *Re C*:

Standing back from all the detail, the reality is that the appellant has no relationship with C, indeed has never even seen him, and that C has now been settled for over two years with the adopters. How can we, how could any judge, take the risk of disturbing that? (*Re C (A Child)* [2013] EWCA Civ 431 [12])

The decision in *Re C* departs significantly from the decision in *Re A and B*.

Whilst *Re A and B* importantly addresses the risk for the child in the long term when making the decision as to whether the child should remain with the adopters, or be placed with his paternal aunt where he can remain within his extended family, the balance sheet approach is applied quite differently.

Mr Justice Holman explains the challenges for members of the judiciary who have responsibility for the difficult task of speculating on what decision to make to ensure that a child's welfare throughout his or her life is achieved:

Advocates, and also judges, often do dismiss points as speculative or speculation. However, in relation to adoption, the Adoption and Children Act 2002 very clearly does require courts (and adoption agencies) to speculate. It requires, as the overarching duty, that the paramount consideration must be the child's welfare throughout his life. This child is still less than two. He is healthy, and his normal life expectancy may be around a further 80 years. It is probable (but speculative) that he and his half sister, F, and his cousin, G, will outlive all the adults in this case by many years. I am required by statute to take a very long term view, but I cannot gaze into a crystal ball. I can only speculate. More specifically, the court is required by section 1(4) (c) of the Act to have regard to 'the likely effect on the child (throughout his life) of having ceased to be a member of the original family and become an adopted person'. Whilst that paragraph requires the court to consider only the 'likely' effect, any such consideration involves speculation; and (speaking generally) the further ahead one looks (and one must envisage a whole lifetime) the more speculative such consideration necessarily becomes. My decision in this case does include speculation. That is what Parliament has told me to do. (*Re A and B v Rotherham Metropolitan Borough Council* [2014] EWFC 47 [17])

Article 8 of the European Convention on Human Rights (ECHR)

The case highlights the range and complexity of rights under Article 8 of the ECHR that should be considered both within pre-proceedings practice but also when a case proceeds to court. When placed for adoption, the child has ceased to be a member of their birth family; a child placed for adoption is similarly enjoying family life where he or she has established very positive relationships and formed strong attachments with the prospective adoptive family. The situation in *Re A and B* highlights the tension between the legal relationship with a biological family, with whom the child has no relationship, and the prospective adopters, who also have a right to respect under Article 8, and where the child has lived for 13 months.

Article 8 is a qualified right and interference is permitted only if it is *necessary* within the meaning of Article 8(2). The court in this instance considered the welfare of the child throughout his life as the paramount consideration, rather than focusing on the competing rights under Article 8:

> If the balance of factors comes down against making an adoption order, then clearly I should not make one. If they are so evenly balanced that it is not possible to say that making an adoption order would be 'better' for him than not doing so, then I should not do so. If, however, the balance does come down clearly in favour of making an adoption order, then, in the circumstances of this case, I should make one. (*Re A and B v Rotherham Metropolitan Borough Council* [2014] EWFC 47 [15])

Mr Justice Holman made the following observation regarding the use of the balance sheet approach that was advocated by Lord Justice Munby in *Re B-S (Children)* [2013]:

> The analogy with balancing scales may be misleading. When weights or objects are put on either side of a scale, their individual precise weights are known, or ascertainable. You can put four objects in one scale pan and seven in the other, and the scales will come down one way or the other due to the aggregate of the individual precise and ascertainable weights on each side. In a case such as this, however, none of the factors have precise weights. All that may be said of any individual factor is that, as a matter of judgment, it is more or less important or weighty than another.
>
> It is not, however, the number of factors which counts but their respective importance. The Adoption and Children Act 2002 does not itself use the language of balance. It requires the court to 'have regard to' all relevant matters, including those specifically referred to in section 1(4). The effect of section 1(6) is that the court must then make a judgment (applying section 1(2) and the paramountcy of welfare throughout the child's life) whether making (in this case) an adoption order 'would be better for the child than not doing so'. (*Re B-S (Children)* [2013] EWCA Civ 1146 [85])

over backwards' to keep the child in the family if at all possible. There is concern that the fact that ours is one of the few countries in Europe which permits adoption notwithstanding parental objection is adding to the uncertainty as to whether adoption can still be put forward as the right and best outcome for a child. (*Re R (A Child)* [2014] EWCA Civ 1625, 16 December 2014 [41])

However, it remains to be seen whether the judgment in *Re R* will reverse the trend from the Supreme Court and Court of Appeal that has cascaded to the lower courts in respect of the challenge to social work assessments. These challenges have been viewed as a further criticism of a profession that has been shoehorned into a target-driven culture that is highly politicized. Social work as a profession has been directed away from the task of engaging with the most complex of family situations to a reliance on an array of experts who have over the last 15 years been given more credence by the court. Furthermore, there has been a significant shift in social work practice away from a helping alliance, formed when social workers engage directly with families, to a distant relationship that is highly prescribed and regulated (Ferguson, 2011).

The distancing in social work has resulted in an increased risk-averse practice with families that has arguably contributed to a continual rise in care figures annually. The recent decline in the number of applications to court should not lead to an illusion that cases are being managed more effectively at the pre-proceedings stage. It simply means there are fewer applications to court, and this may be more akin to the fear of being challenged by the court rather than on the success of the modernization agenda of the family court, with more robust assessment and planning at the pre-proceedings stage. The practice reality remains unchanged and the pre-proceedings space is largely invisible.

CHAPTER 6

Challenges for Practice

Dealing with Complex Issues that Increase Risk for Children within a Family Justice System

Introduction

Professionals working in child protection require knowledge, skill and expertise to deal with complex issues that demand face-to-face contact and communication with children and their families. We have explored in previous chapters the challenges facing professionals who are tasked with navigating an increasingly target-driven culture with no corresponding increase in resources (Featherstone *et al.*, 2014). Furthermore, we have identified the complexities around both private and public law proceedings that involve children, and highlighted in the most complex of cases the move towards a remote control approach to working with the most vulnerable children and their families on behalf of both professionals and the courts. This chapter focuses on the urgent need to refocus on the child and the consequences for children if they are not prioritized within a system that purports to hold the child as the focus, but where in practice the reality is quite different.

Where professionals are working under such considerable pressure, the quality of assessments often falls short of a standard that is acceptable to the court, as is evidenced in the case of *Re B-S (Children)* [2013], which has been discussed in some detail in the preceding chapter, requiring no further need to rehearse the salient ratio of the case or indeed judicial comment.

Notwithstanding judicial scrutiny in several high-profile cases since 2013 that have been critical of the quality of analysis in the evidence presented to the court, the consequences for children when assessments are not sufficiently detailed can never be underestimated. This chapter considers some of the indicators that result in serious injury or death to a child, and provides strategies for professionals who are working with children to ensure they remain firmly central in the family justice system. Despite the principle enshrined in the Children Act 1989 that the welfare of the child is paramount, the system still remains largely adult focused (Holt, 2014a).

Serious injuries and child deaths: lessons to be learned

The tragic death of Daniel Pelka on 3 March 2012 is the most recent high-profile child death, following a number of previous cases which highlight the complex circumstances that avoid detection by a range of agencies responsible for the protection of children. Daniel was aged four years and eight months when he was admitted to hospital having suffered a cardiac arrest. He was pronounced dead within an hour of arriving at hospital dehydrated and weighing 10.7 kg (1.68 st).

Following examination Daniel was found to be malnourished, with an acute subdural haematoma to the right side of his head, and evidence of older, mild subdural haematoma of several months' or years' duration, together with several bruises on his body. Daniel was one of three children of a family who had migrated to Coventry from Poland in 2005. During the period 2005–2008 Daniel's father remained with the family before his return to Poland. The family were known to safeguarding agencies, as the police responded to

27 reports of domestic abuse. Concerns were raised about alcohol and substance abuse, with Daniel's mother admitted to hospital following a substance overdose. There were concerns also that Daniel's mother was suffering from depression. The police concluded that the children were not aware of the violence, as they had not directly witnessed it.

Because of their immigration status the family were unable to claim welfare benefits, which resulted both in frequent house moves owing to financial difficulties and in eviction. The family were clearly living in poverty, with a lifestyle that was described as chaotic – in part at least as a direct result of the family's immigration status, and also agencies' response to families who are complex. Professional assessments failed to analyse and reflect upon the complexities of this family and the impact this would have on the children.

Notwithstanding the fact that Daniel was withdrawn and solemn at school, with poor language development, little interaction with other children and significant developmental delay, these concerns were not recognized or recorded as signs of neglect. Nor were they considered as part of a child protection referral that may have prompted a more detailed assessment of the family, including reports from the police. Despite being known to services and exhibiting signs of developmental delay, Daniel had become an invisible child. The children of this family, including a brother who was aged seven when Daniel died, had become lost, with information largely provided by the mother and taken at face value and without the necessary probing and analysis that may have resulted in Daniel being referred to the local authority. Brandon *et al.* (2008) highlight a common feature in most serious case reviews that is known as 'disguised compliance', whereby parents have the ability to draw professionals attention away from allegations of harm.

Following Daniel's death the reality of life for Daniel was uncovered. Daniel had been regularly subjected to physical harm and deliberate starvation. As a punishment for stealing food he was forced to eat salt, made to sit in a cold bath and locked in a room with no door handle. The conditions in Daniel's bedroom were significantly below a standard that was acceptable for any child, and no professional ever witnessed the conditions that Daniel was living in. Routine appointments with a range of professionals and agencies were missed and there was no sharing of information. The serious case review that was held following the death of Daniel raised concerns about the lack of communication, poor record keeping and assumptions being made around culture and language.

On 31 July 2013, Daniel's mother and her partner were found guilty of the murder of Daniel and sentenced to a minimum of 30 years each. Both have since been found dead in prison.

The review did not blame or identify any individual agency but sadly highlighted recurrent features found in the majority of serious case reviews. First, the professionals involved were relying on the rule of optimism; they were reassured and owing to volume of work, moved on to the next case. Second, the absence of a chronology and analysis would have assisted a more detailed understanding of the family history (Wannacott and Watts, 2014).

The tragic death of Daniel Pelka provides important learning for professionals working in child protection.

Effective approaches for protecting children
1. The child must never be invisible

The importance of keeping the child at the heart of good child protection practice must be central. Learning messages from research into serious case reviews, such as Daniel Pelka, provides important evidence as to the problems when children do not remain at the heart of the child protection system (Ofsted, 2011; DfE, 2015d). Much of this book has highlighted the pitfalls with an increasing move towards the digitization and procedural nature of agencies and organizations operating within the public sector, which has resulted in a remote control approach to practice. Notwithstanding these pressures, professionals who are tasked to work within child protection must reclaim their skills in working with children, and be in a position to have a holistic picture of the child and their family. This will be achieved by a deep analysis of the needs, wishes and feelings of the child from direct knowledge, and not upon a reliance on third-party information. Pivotal is the need for participation to be a process rather than an event. Listening to and working closely with children has to be based on sound theoretical understanding, a child-centred philosophy supported with practical skills, good supervision and appropriate and regular training. (Lefevre, 2014).

As a starting point, social workers need to have an understanding of what children are able or not able to do or understand at different ages. Knowledge of child development and an ability to apply this to practice is absolutely essential in the social work assessment of a child's development – highlighting delay or regression. In addition, it is crucial to understand age-appropriate play and what concepts/ideas children may understand. Fahlberg (1981, 1991) provides consistently clear and helpful guidance in these areas; both works are detailed but they also provide an accessible understanding of a child's physical, social and emotional needs and development. A working knowledge of attachment theory is essential. Children who are in contact with children's social care are likely to be suffering difficulties around attachment, loss and separation. Aldgate and Simmonds (1988) emphasize that it is almost impossible to understand the impact of separation without a good understanding of attachment theory. Central to understanding how the theory links with practice is direct contact with the child, who must always remain at the core of the system. Resource constraints must never be a reason not to prioritize direct contact with the child in their own environment. The importance of meeting with, observing and hearing the child cannot be underestimated, yet all too often this takes secondary place to organizational demands on practitioner time (Ferguson, 2011).

2. Professionals need to be engaged, not merely involved, with the child

Children are insufficiently consulted or spoken with – siblings of the index child and young people living outside of the home are not interviewed or assessed. Social workers fall short when assessing children with complex needs/disabilities, often focusing on the disability and parent's capacity to cope rather than assessing what is *good enough* for this particular child, who may require a higher standard of care. The higher standard of care may of course be very good for a child without complex needs, but for children who experience a range of vulnerabilities the same standard of care may be just *good enough*. No apologies are made for stating that child protection procedures and practices must protect the most vulnerable of children for them to be effective. If our procedures and practices do not protect children with the most complex needs, they are not working (Ofsted, 2012). In respect of older children, practitioners often consider them to be *hard to help*. Young people are also vulnerable and may be *hard to reach*, but we must reach them and find ways of engaging them in assessments (Lefevre, 2010).

Professional involvement with the child is not the same as engagement. Just because another professional is involved with a child and their family does not necessarily mean that they are proactively engaged with protecting the child. The danger is that we assume that if a child has a social worker, they are being protected; or if a police officer has visited the house after a domestic violence incident, the child is safe. The crucially important issue here is to always check information – children are best protected when information is shared between the professionals engaged with the child and when any action is coordinated. Professionals must never assume that someone else is engaged and responding to the concerns. If professionals have concerns about a child, they need to take action – it is always preferable that two professionals take action rather than no one at all.

3. Information cannot be accepted at face value

The ability to elicit a detailed family history that contributes to a holistic understanding of the child and their family, including an understanding of parenting behaviours, is pivotal to a good assessment. However, it is often absent when examining documentation following the death or serious injury of a child. It is important to know about the parents' or other caregivers' history – including their own experience of being parented, and past and potential patterns of behaviour or concerns – to identify factors which may point to enhanced risk or which may be protective. In addition, it is important to assess the impact on the parent of behaviours in the wider family network. In circumstances whereby families are overwhelmed and struggling with a range of complex factors, this does not necessarily rule out the capacity to change, but it will require potential or actual risk factors to be identified that may present harm to a child, and a plan of work to be undertaken to assess whether the risk can be reduced.

Past history is a good indicator of future behaviour, and it is crucial that social workers obtain a full and detailed history of parenting behaviour and make an analysis of the information in terms of risk to the child (Broadhurst *et al.*, 2009).

We have discussed the invisibility of children, but in order to obtain a holistic assessment of the family, men and fathers must never be allowed to remain invisible in the process. It is not sufficient to involve men and fathers only when they are implicated in the suspected abuse of a child. Gilligan *et al.* (2011) suggest a need for change in the approach to involving fathers more routinely in the child protection system. Perceptions of men as *troublesome* in the context of child protection is a prevailing feature; their absence, for example, is usually interpreted negatively rather than examined in the context of how professionals may positively target women and ignore men. Assessments must always include men and consider how fathers can play an important role in the lives of children. In respect of men who are regarded as troublesome, there is a need to examine how organizations respond to men who present a risk but who may be hard to reach (Reissman and Quinney, 2005).

4. Parental participation is not the same as cooperation

Practitioners often confuse parental participation as a sign of cooperation. Whilst participation is important, it should never be mistaken for the willingness to both recognize the concerns raised by professionals and accept the need to change the behaviour that is resulting in an unacceptable level of harm to the child. The rule of optimism has been the focus in a significant number of serious case reviews (Brandon *et al.*, 2012). Unless there is clear evidence to suggest the risk to the child is reduced, professionals cannot assume parental participation will result in positive outcomes for the child. In a climate of remote control practice, and the overriding need to keep the regulatory machine functioning, the rule of optimism is more likely to feature when professionals feel under pressure of increasing timescales and targets but with no corresponding increase in resources to focus on really engaging with children and their families. The rule of optimism rationalizes evidence that contradicts the reality for the child: even where the facts evidence an increase in risk, professionals convince themselves and others that the opposite is true. Where there is any suspicion that practitioners may be relying on the rule of optimism, there is an urgent need to analyse and critically reflect on the evidence, and be really clear about objectives and outcomes for the child and their family (Holt, 2014a).

The importance of regular and effective supervision is crucial in these situations, and practitioners must have the time to reflect on their engagement with the child and their family with experienced supervisors who need to probe further where there are concerns that the rule of optimism is being used (Eastman, 2014).

5. Neglect is a neglected issue

Neglect is damaging to children in the short and long term. Neglect is associated with some of the poorest outcomes. It affects children in the early years, but teenage neglect – often overlooked – is also damaging. Formulating an effective response to neglect still poses national and local challenges (Daniel, Burgess and Scott, 2012). Neglect is identified as a significant issue. Although it is rarely the cause of death, it is a feature in the majority of cases where children are killed or seriously harmed: 'Neglect was an underlying feature in at least 60% of the serious case reviews. Past or present neglect was a factor in eleven out of fourteen suicide cases' (Brandon *et al.*, 2012, p.3).

Importantly, evidence of neglect may provide an important signal of a poor relationship between the parent and child. Essential to understanding neglect is the recognition that it originates from parents who are not sufficiently prioritizing the child's basic needs. It is primarily, therefore, a relationship issue that involves intentional and continued abuse of a child. Often professionals wait for an incident to trigger action to protect the child, and therefore the child has often been experiencing harm for a significant period of time. It is essential that practitioners establish what value the parent places on their child, and how aware the parent is of the child's needs, personality, strengths and struggles. It is crucial when assessing risk to identify priorities for parents, in terms of their ability to meet both their own needs and the needs of their child (Howe, 2005).

Horwath and Morrison (2001) developed a model for assessing capacity and willingness to change, which remains a good reference guide for practitioners when assessing both capacity and motivation to change:

1. 'Genuine commitment' where parents make good efforts to change and show commitment to improving their parenting for the benefit of the children. There is unlikely to be a requirement for compulsory measures.

2. 'Tokenism' where parents express commitment to change, but for a range of possible reasons do not put in the actual effort to change. There may be need for compulsory measures, although the parents may be able to accept that the care is not good enough.

3. 'Compliance imitation' or 'approval seeking' where there can be high effort to make changes (perhaps sporadically) but the commitment to sustained change is not demonstrated. There

may not be a requirement for compulsory measures if, perhaps, the parents are able to come to an acceptance that the child requires alternative care or that there is an ongoing need for extensive additional support for the child within the home.

4. 'Dissent' or 'avoidance' where there is a combination of low effort and low commitment, and where compulsory measures are highly likely to be required.

5. Given the individual variability and complexity of children's circumstances, it may be better to accept that for every situation there will need to be assessment, discussion with the family and negotiation between professionals in order to establish the level of unmet need, the associated risk of harm and the extent of real opportunity for change without the need for compulsory measures, or indeed with compulsory measures.

(Daniel, Burgess and Scott, 2012, p.56)

Importantly, intervention by professionals where neglect is an issue needs to be concrete, comprehensive, sustained and brokered by effective relationships that are both clear and honest about the positive aspects, but also identifying the risks (Daniel, Taylor and Scott, 2011).

6. Think the unthinkable

Adopting a healthy scepticism is important when engaging with families where children may be at risk. Whilst it is clearly important to seek parental accounts of how their children are looked after when undertaking an assessment, it is not always the most reliable way of establishing an accurate or complete assessment of what is happening within the home or the lived experiences of the child. It is important to spend time observing parents with their children within the home to assess the quality of interaction in terms of play, setting boundaries and making meals. Investing in this time with the family will facilitate a deeper knowledge and understanding of the family and the relationships (Holt, 2014a).

The message from research informs us that 75 per cent of parents do not cooperate with services, which includes disguised compliance and telling professionals what they want to hear. It is therefore crucial that professionals probe further when they have concerns that a child is at risk of suffering harm (Brandon *et al.*, 2012).

7. Assessment is a process, not an event

Undertaking a good assessment relies upon a deep understanding of the current context of the family and that of the chronology of past experiences, both strengths and struggles. A thorough understanding of the overall context, both past and present, allows the professional to use the information to make decisions about what help is required to ensure improved outcomes for the child. The family history must always be used to inform current decision making. The historical information will provide insight into the child's lived experiences, and a good chronology is child focused (Brown and Ward, 2013). Often chronologies resemble lists of events – usually where the family or child is struggling – and they have been used to gather evidence where there are child protection concerns (Holt, 2014a). It would be interesting to see how a chronology would read if it was written from the child's perspective in respect of their accounts, wishes and feelings.

Assessments are fluid not fixed and are changing regularly as new situations and circumstances emerge (Brown and Ward, 2013). In complex families these changes are even more frequent and this in itself is noteworthy. A good assessment requires negotiation and cooperation with other professionals who are engaged with the family. Professionals from a range of agencies will have knowledge, skills and expertise that will inform a deeper understanding of the child and their family. It is crucially important to see, listen to and hear the child (Daniel, Taylor and Scott, 2011).

with complex families. Fixed thinking and group think often reflect an over-focusing on descriptive material and a lack of analysis of the situation as a whole (Kelly, 2002; Sidebotham 2012; Sidebotham, Golding and ALSPAC, 2001; Sinclair and Bullock 2002).

Repeat removals: the revolving-door response to fixed thinking

Fixed thinking is clearly a barrier to understanding a child's changing circumstances, and arguably features in an important area of child care/legal practice, which may provide some insight into the prevalence of multiple repeat removals of children from their parents.

Multiple repeat removals from birth parents presents a challenge for professionals and it highlights the plight of mothers, in particular, who experience successive repeat removals of their children. Broadhurst and Mason (2013) signal a lack of post-removal support services, together with pre-birth assessments, that reflect a reinforcing of fixed thinking in relation to forensic historical evidence, rather than providing the practical and emotional support that may elicit a quite different outcome for parents. The changes introduced following the reforms of the family justice system focus on achieving swift decisions once a case progresses to court. In practice, if professionals have not engaged effectively with mothers/ parents at the pre-proceedings stage, there will be almost no scope to do this once an application to court has been made. It is likely, therefore, that for some parents early fixed thinking by a range of professionals could ultimately result in a revolving door, where the focus is on risk-averse practice in a climate of timescales and targets.

Shaw *et al.* (2014) and Harwin *et al.* (2014) report that during the period of their study, from 2007 to 2013, more than 7000 birth mothers and 23,000 children appeared in successive repeat removal care proceedings. It is also likely that this figure underestimates an accurate picture, as reliable data was not available prior to 2007.

One of the most revealing aspects of this study is the intervals between successive care proceedings, which allow little opportunity for mothers in particular to evidence the changes required to shift the thinking of professionals and the court. Thus, in 42 per cent of cases, the court made an order close to a child's birth. Fixed thinking amongst a range of professionals, together with shorter timescales to complete care proceedings, leaves little or no scope for some of the most vulnerable mothers to make the changes necessary or to escape the cycle of repeat removals of their children. The social and economic costs cannot be underestimated.

Case study

Refer back to the case study outlined in Chapter 1 and considered in each of the preceding chapters. Reflecting on the issues identified in this chapter in respect of the family history, the multiple risks and successive repeat removals, consider:

- the challenges for professionals working with Kelly, Hassan and Bertie to ensure that organizational imperatives are not prioritized above the needs of Bertie and his family

- the role of fixed thinking in decision-making processes

- the importance of effective supervision in providing an appropriate challenge.

Discussion

The complexity of achieving a holistic assessment as expressed in *Re B-S* is highlighted in this chapter. The difficulties for many parents are complex, and there is a tension for professionals navigating this difficult terrain between protecting the rights of children to be safe (Gupta and Lloyd-Jones, 2014) and ensuring that parents have sufficient time to make the changes necessary to reduce the risk for their children. Practice is not located within a vacuum – the government drive to increase the number of children placed for adoption was given legislative support in the Children and Families Act 2014, and local authorities are under pressure to support adoption for a number of reasons, including economic and regulatory.

First, placing a child for adoption is economically more sustainable for local authorities in a climate of austerity and severe cuts to funding. Second, the DfE publish the number of children local authorities have placed for adoption (DfE, 2014a). The impact for local authorities of an audit culture around adoption cannot be underestimated – achieving targets that are in the public domain is completely at odds with the judicial comment from both the Supreme Court and Court of Appeal in *Re B and Re B-S*, where a decision to place a child for adoption must be based on a holistic and analytical assessment of the child and their family. Members of the judiciary are clearly advocating that professionals need to be dealing with the challenges facing families, some of which are highlighted in this chapter, at the earliest opportunity. Although the judiciary have not named professional fixed thinking in terms of permanency planning for children, it is evident that this is a feature in many decisions, which is supported and reinforced by successive government policy. Decision making that is located within a climate of a less tolerant approach to welfare can easily position poor parents, usually women, with adoptive parents who will provide economic security for the child and an acceptable level of risk that supports the policy ideal (Featherstone, Morris and White, 2013).

It is essential that professionals faced with such challenges, both political and judicial, create and develop a culture of learning and challenging. There is an urgent need for front-line professionals to reconfigure in order to enable more time for the necessary face-to-face contact with children and their families who turn to a system at times of stress and when they are most in need. Furthermore, organizations need to recognize and respond to the need for effective supervision that enables practitioners to reflect and analyse assessments, which should be an ongoing process rather than a one-off event. The focus of all assessments should be on needs, rather than resource led, and professionals need to be supported to develop the confidence to challenge organizational imperatives in favour of ensuring that the rights of children and their families are protected (Eastman, 2014).

CHAPTER 7

Findings from Research

Pre-proceedings Practice

Introduction

As an experienced social worker of 30 years, a qualified barrister of 10 years and an academic of 11 years practising and researching in the area of child protection and family law, I am able to claim with a degree of authority a unique lens (Rapoport, 1986) on a changing landscape in child protection practice.

There is no doubt that within judicial care proceedings there have been serious concerns about significant delays in decision making, and the consequences for children and their families are well documented (Holt *et al.*, 2014; Masson *et al.*, 2013). The challenges of avoiding unnecessary delays have been the subject of much debate, with legal and social work communities attributing responsibility to each other (MOJ, 2011a, 2011b). With the creation and implementation of the Public Law Outline in 2008 (intended to front-load more rigorous social work into pre-proceedings practice) and with the reduction in duration of care proceedings to 26 weeks, it was hoped that cases that proceeded to court might be resolved more quickly, and – overall – risks and delays for children and families would be reduced.

The motivation to probe the landscape of pre-proceedings practice arose from an analysis of an ethnographic study of pre-proceedings meetings between the years 2009 and 2011 (Broadhurst *et al.*, 2012).

Furthermore, the study represents the first major theoretical and empirical exploration of pre-proceedings practice in child protection *as it occurs*. This chapter explores the tensions in public law child care proceedings following the introduction of the Public Law Outline (MOJ, 2008), by examining two pertinent issues that arise from the implementation of the Public Law Outline (PLO) (2008), the Practice Direction 36C (2013), the revised Public Law Outline (2014) and the Children and Families Act, which became law on 22 April 2014.

First, the chapter explores the boundary of decision making for children and families when decisions are increasingly moved into an administrative rather than a judicial space (Holt and Kelly, 2012b). Second, in a climate of austerity, limited resources and tighter timescales for cases when they are in court, consideration is given as to the type, availability and quality of advocacy and representation to support children and their parents in the changing landscape of pre-proceedings protocols and practice (Masson, 2012). A brief summary of the issues and findings is presented below.

The research into pre-proceedings practice over a five-year period examines the reality of pre-proceedings practice as it occurs within the child protection process (Broadhurst *et al.*, 2012; Holt *et al.*, 2013b). It has included observations of pre-proceedings meetings, analysis of case files and minutes of pre-proceedings meetings, interviews with social work practitioners and managers, interviews with members of the legal profession and family court advisors and the shadowing of a family court judge. This has allowed the development of a unique lens (Rapoport, 1986) on the reality of a pre-proceedings protocol and has allowed the opportunity to make a significant contribution to the debate in terms of what the protocol actually means for children and families.

It is argued that the deadline of 26 weeks when cases progress to court, and a formal pre-proceedings protocol, are not the answer to ensuring effective social work practice and optimal outcomes for children and families. The pre-proceedings protocol runs in parallel with, or more usually towards the end of, a child protection process, and introduces increased bureaucracy and procedure. This leaves social workers and families confused as to where, when and by whom decisions are being made (Morris, 2013). Within pre-proceedings protocols and practice, important decisions are being made without the oversight of the court (Masson *et al.*, 2013). Whilst the PLO formally allowed parents the opportunity to access legal advice in pre-proceedings, it is proposed that, even where advocacy is available and accessed by families, the quality and availability of good advocacy is at best patchy, and is now further threatened by cuts to legal aid (Pearce, Masson and Bader, 2011). My interpretation is that the rationale for changes to policy and practice with regard to the timetable for the child are simply rhetoric. Whilst court costs may be reduced, there is likely to be spillage elsewhere with children potentially left at risk for a longer period of time prior to an application to court being made (Dickens, 2012).

Background

Decision making in the context of child protection practice has traditionally been located within the local authority with involvement from other agencies/organizations who have a duty in law to offer support (Ferguson, 2004). This unitary system of child protection under the Children Act 1989 may not be without its faults, but recent changes to policy and legislation (DfE, 2014b; MOJ, 2008; MOJ and DfE, 2012; and the Children and Families Act 2014) have introduced further layers of procedure. This has resulted in additional resources being required to operate in what seem to be two systems working, at best, in parallel. At a time when child protection services are already stretched beyond capacity, it would appear that introducing further instrumental approaches in order to achieve targets and reduce costs is an ill-conceived plan (Morris and Featherstone, 2010).

On 31 March 2013, there were 382,400 children in need in England, a rate of 325.7 per 10,000 children. Approximately 60,000 child protection conferences were held in England in the period

2012–2013, and 52,700 children were the subject of a child protection plan. There were a total of 68,110 children in care on 31 March 2013 (DfE, 2013). Figures for 31 March 2015 indicate a slight increase in the number of children in need, 391,000; the number of children who are the subject of an initial child protection conference has risen to 160,150, with 49,700 children subject to a child protection plan, and an increase in the number of children in care to 69,540 (DfE, 2015e, 2015f). This highlights that cases within pre-proceedings and care proceedings are only part of the story. The concern is that when further procedures are introduced into an already fragile context of child protection practice, the emphasis on procedure eclipses the benefits of establishing effective working relationships with families (White, Morris and Featherstone, 2014).

My intention is not to simplify what is a deeply complex area of child protection practice; but the system prior to the introduction of the PLO (2008) was at least clear and transparent. Social workers, supported by colleagues from other agencies, worked together when a child was either suffering harm or there was a likelihood of future harm (Parton, 2014b). Assessments of the child and their family through effective multi-agency working helped to inform the decision as to whether the child was at risk and therefore whether or not the child was in need of a child protection plan (DfE, 2013).

Commentators such as Featherstone, Broadhurst and Holt (2012) suggest that the system of child protection within the UK is already too instrumental and business focused. However, my contention here is that whilst this may be accurate, many children are nevertheless supported effectively with child protection plans that allow them to remain living within their own immediate or extended family (Shaw *et al.*, 2014).

The focus of good child protection practice is to assess and manage risk and to provide protection to some of the most vulnerable children and young people (Frost and Parton, 2009). Therefore, it is inevitable that in some circumstances following an assessment of the child and their family, a decision is made that the risk for the child

specifically the decision-making process for children and their families within pre-proceedings protocols. The research began with an ethnographic study between the years 2009 and 2011 (Broadhurst *et al.*, 2012). In this study, activities were observed in social work offices, home visits, legal advice-giving and pre-proceedings meetings. Interviews with professionals and families were also undertaken. This was a unique piece of research aimed at exploring and understanding the operationalization of a pre-proceedings protocol almost immediately after the PLO (2008). Findings highlighted that there was injustice occurring in pre-proceedings meetings for children and families. Thus, the second aspect of the empirical work was undertaken where a family court advisor was introduced into pre-proceedings with the aim of exploring whether bolstering pre-proceedings processes with additional resources would be effective in ensuring justice for children and families and in diverting cases away from court where it is safe and appropriate to do so (Holt *et al.*, 2013a, 2013b).

Pivotal to the work is an exploration of how legislation, policy and practice are operationalized, understood and experienced by multiple stakeholders. There is no one single approach to the collection or analysis of data; rather a mixed methods approach is adopted (Teddlie and Tashakkori, 2010). Whilst recognizing the theoretical tensions and debates of such an approach, the work draws on the 'pragmatic view' that the research question is of primary importance. Techniques grounded in both positivism and interpretivism can be used best to explore a question layered in complexity: from understanding developments in policy and practice guidance; understanding organizational experiences of operationalizing legislation; understanding contextual and structural influences on decision making; and understanding individual experiences operating at different levels within pre-proceedings protocols (Wetherell, 1998).

At one level there has been an ongoing analysis of the development of legislation, policy and practice guidance. From this has emerged a strand of discussion around the discourses implicit in the development of the pre-proceedings protocol, for example discourses around the timetable for the child, rights and responsibilities and economic discourses (Holt *et al.*, 2014).

At a second level, empirical data collection took place within a number of practice settings that involved extensive negotiation with, and access to, cases within several local authorities; it has employed quantitative and qualitative methods and has been disseminated at local, national and international level. Two projects have involved data collection in seven sites. The second project developed the methodological approach and explored further the findings from the first project. Importantly, this second project introduced a family court advisor into pre-proceedings work to consider the potential impact on practice, assessment of risk and outcomes for children and families.

Initial project: explorations of practice in pre-proceedings meetings in four local authorities, 2009–2011

This study culminated in four important findings in pre-proceedings practice. First, the dominant frame of decision making in pre-proceedings meetings was that of the local authority. Decisions were driven almost exclusively by a local authority agenda, and children and families had little opportunity to question or input effectively to decision making. Second, the child was almost 'invisible' in the pre-proceedings meetings. There was no sense of the voice of the child or of their wishes. The absence of the voice of the child within the child protection system is further supported in the findings from a study undertaken by La Valle, Payne and Jelicic in 2012. Third, there was a tension between practitioners around where the boundary of decision making fell. Most children were already subject to a child protection plan, and decisions made at the child protection conference/ core group were not addressed in the pre-proceedings meeting and vice versa. Fourth, confusion at pre-proceedings meetings was compounded where legal representatives for families were present. There was no independent representation for children and where advocates were present their contribution was at best patchy.

Outline of the study

An initial pilot study in four local authorities was undertaken between the years 2009 and 2011. This ethnographic study aimed to evaluate the impact of front-loading cases in the pre-proceedings stage. During this period one day a week was spent observing what were then referred to as legal gateway meetings (now following the PLO (2008), formally pre-proceedings meetings). Observations in social work offices and home visits were also undertaken. Social work practitioners, managers, lawyers, independent reviewing officers and parents were interviewed as part of this study, and three weeks were spent shadowing a designated family judge in one local authority to observe how cases were processed once an application to court was made.

Method

In this work, transcriptions of 12 pre-proceedings meetings were produced verbatim. After several readings of that data by all researchers, subsections were then transcribed in more detail according to the usual conventions of conversational analysis (developed by Jefferson, 2004). The focus on certain aspects of the data for more detailed transcription can be considered usual in conversation analysis (Bazeley, 2013). Each team member worked on the same transcript individually before meeting together to discuss the work. This achieved early consistency in coding and interpretation of the data. This was not an attempt to produce 'reliability'; rather it was an acknowledged process between the team to create a rigorous and transparent journey towards an argument built on clear and comprehensive evidence.

In terms of analysis this first study employed the micro-analysis of talk. This allowed the examination of real-time interaction in the quasi-legal setting of the pre-proceedings meeting, getting closer to the realities of practice (Todd and Fisher, 1993; Wetherell, 1998). Through a focus on the structure and content of conversation we can get close to the substance of competing definitions and claims *in situ*, exploring the possibilities for institutional alignment with service users (Drew and Heritage, 1992). The analysis provided rich insights into the difficulties professionals encounter when trying to achieve consensual solutions for children outside the court arena (Broadhurst *et al.*, 2012).

The study conforms to internationally accepted ethical guidelines. Ethical approval was obtained from the home institution, and all participants in the study gave verbal consent (ESRC, 2010).

Findings

Four important findings emerged from this study. First, the rhetoric of policy and the reality for children and families are not always the same; within agencies/organizations, it is the dominant frame that informs judgement, decisions and actions that have a significant impact on the way other organizations/individuals are perceived or respond (Broadhurst *et al.*, 2011; Goffman, 1983). Overall it was evident that the dominant frame of decision making was that of the local authority. Decisions were driven almost exclusively by a local authority agenda, and children and families had little opportunity to question or input effectively to decision making.

Second, there was concern about the visibility and wishes and needs of children in these pre-proceedings meetings where decisions were being made without the oversight of the court. In reality, the children remained almost entirely invisible – the meeting was attended by adults, and focused almost exclusively on the ability of adults to make the necessary changes expected of them by the local authority. The child was often addressed by name only and I left the majority of meetings without any knowledge or understanding of the particular needs or wishes of the child.

Third, there was clear tension amongst practitioners as to where the boundary fell between the decisions and recommendations of the child protection conference, core group meeting and the pre-proceedings meeting. In most cases, children's social care had a lengthy previous involvement with the family, and in the majority of cases children had been subject to a child protection plan for at least two years. Despite the majority of children being the subject of a current child protection plan, the pre-proceedings protocol was operated in parallel to the child protection conference and planning and the two systems worked entirely separately. Decisions that were made within the child protection conference were not addressed in the pre-proceedings meeting and vice versa. This was confusing for both practitioners and families who were uncertain about the boundaries of decision making and how these should be communicated and managed (Holt *et al.*, 2013b).

Finally, confusion was compounded when legal representatives arrived at the pre-proceedings meeting. They were often unable to comprehend what they were expected to do or how they should perform, and they were largely silent. Importantly, there was no separate and/or independent representation for children within the pre-proceedings meetings. Whilst advocacy for parents was available, it was observed to be at best patchy. A detailed discussion about the role of advocacy within the pre-proceedings meeting falls outside of the scope of this book, but is detailed in Holt *et al.* (2013b). It is important to note that in almost all meetings observed, legal representatives for parents were unfamiliar as to what to do, operating within a terrain largely dominated by the local authority. There was very little evidence of active brokering by legal representatives on behalf of parents, even when decisions that were being made seemed to be unfair, unjust and without detailed consultation.

Second project: evaluation of the impact of introducing a family court advisor into pre-proceedings practice

At the pre-proceedings stage a family court advisor can focus the pre-proceedings meeting around the needs and wishes of the children; can broker more effective relationships with parents; can offer additional advice and support for social workers in terms of plans of action and assessment of children and families; and can have a 'headstart' should a case go into proceedings, thus potentially reducing delays in the court process. In some cases where contributions from the family court advisor were taken on board and where they were not later challenged in court there did appear to be more robust assessments and decision making, and fewer delays for children and families. However, in other cases courts continued to demand further assessments of families, thus delays were compounded. Findings suggest that most effective practice and consequent outcomes for children and families occur when all stakeholders in child protection, from individual social workers to the judiciary, work together to plan whole systemic change (Forrester, 2013). It is crucial to note that in all cases the resources needed to engage in rigorous pre-proceedings practice are significant.

Outline of the study

The 'Evaluation of the Early Intervention of the Family Court Advisor in Pre-Proceedings Work with Children and Families', commissioned by Cafcass, was highlighted in the recent Family Justice Review (MOJ, 2011a) as an important ongoing piece of research exploring ways in which pre-proceedings decision making involving the welfare of children and families on the 'edge of care' might be more effective. This project has been extended from the initial pilot areas of Coventry and Warwickshire (Holt, Kelly, Broadhurst, Doherty and Yeend, 2013) to Liverpool (Holt *et al.*, 2014).

Method

In this work, alongside the analysis of case file documents, semi-structured interviews are analysed using the flexible technique of thematic analysis (Braun and Clarke, 2006), whereby patterns and themes within and across data are identified, analysed and reported. With regard to the case files a template was agreed by all researchers in terms of the information required from the documents. This ensured consistency and transparency and was a collection of data concerning the context of cases and, as the projects progressed, structural issues pertinent to analysis – for example, family composition; presenting issues; presence of legal representation at pre-proceedings meetings; and the timeframe from the initial point of contact with children's social care to the resolution of the case, through either successful rehabilitation within the child's birth family or application to court for a care order. Minutes of pre-proceedings meetings were analysed using a thematic analysis.

The interviews were transcribed verbatim, and after individual coding the team met together to discuss initial analysis, transparency and consistency. As with much qualitative research this was an iterative process, and regular meetings afforded the opportunity to probe and discuss emergent themes.

The third pilot site (Liverpool) built on learning from Coventry and Warwickshire, and whilst data collection has only recently been completed, the project gained significant momentum and attracted considerable ministerial and judicial interest. It has been interesting to observe practice as policy and national guidelines evolve for reducing delays should child care cases progress to court.

The study conforms to internationally accepted ethical guidelines. Ethical approval was obtained from the home institution, and all participants in the study gave verbal consent.

Findings

The findings from the Coventry and Warwickshire pilot and the Liverpool site are now published (Holt, Kelly, Broadhurst, Doherty and Yeend, 2013; Holt *et al.*, 2014). In this study the most experienced family court advisors were recruited to the project, and the experience and expertise was helpful in a number of ways: brokering more effective relationships with parents; suggesting additional assessment work; gaining a 'headstart' should a case progress to court, therefore reducing replication and delays for children and families; and, importantly, representing the voice of the child. It was apparent in the earlier work that legal representation at the pre-proceedings meetings suffered from problems similar to those in stage one (Holt, Kelly, Broadhurst, Doherty and Yeend, 2013).

Whilst replicating some of the findings of the Coventry and Warwickshire study, I would argue that the most important impact of rolling the study out to Liverpool was the considerable investment by multiple stakeholders at the outset of the project. Thorough negotiations and planning prior to the commencement of the evaluative stage of the research meant that the authority committed significant resources to implementing a pre-proceedings protocol in a highly rigorous, transparent and consistent manner. The pre-proceedings protocol was driven by a judicial commitment to resolving cases in court within the 26-weeks time limit, and whilst there are serious concerns about the implications of this for children and families, the pre-proceedings practice represents a thorough understanding of the need for detailed systemic planning for change.

Notwithstanding the potential positive impact of the role of the family court advisor in pre-proceedings it has to be recognized that the work is in the context of 'proportionate working' and can only be one part of a whole complex system that must consider working practices across all agencies and organizations.

Discussion

It is my contention that introducing a statutory time limit of 26 weeks for the completion of public law child care cases is an attempt to ensure compliance with court targets, thus reducing costs, and is nothing to do with the rhetoric of the timetable for the child. In practice, the tightening of timescales within the court will only result in spillage elsewhere. Moreover, the Bar Council (2012) and Holt (2014) have expressed concern that if issues are not sufficiently explored and all the options considered, this could lead to miscarriages of justice. Importantly, the child could be left holding the risk for longer before a case finally proceeds to court and thereby will wait longer for a permanent placement to be found upon conclusion of the court proceedings.

Recent judgments from the Supreme Court and Court of Appeal, notably *Re B (A Child)* [2013], *Re B-S (Children)* [2013], *Re G (A Child)* [2013] and *Re E (A Child)* [2014], suggest that there should be a move away from linear decision making to holistic assessments and planning for children (Masson, 2014). In relation to pre-proceedings protocols and practice, the judgment of Lord Justice McFarlane in *Re G* is of particular relevance. Lord Justice McFarlane raises the important issue of the '*least worst outcome*' for the child. If we start at an attempt at rehabilitation with the family, the least worst outcome is adoption. If, however, we start at adoption the least worst outcome could be rehabilitation with the family. It could be argued that moving important decision making to the pre-proceedings stage in an attempt to divert cases away from court may in effect promote this linear approach to decision making – an approach of 'We have tried rehabilitation, that has not succeeded, so the least worst option for the child is adoption.' It could be argued that an early steer from the court, so in effect cases proceed to court at a much earlier stage, could potentially facilitate an increased number of children returning permanently to live with their family (Masson, 2014).

It appears convincing that achieving holistic assessments as outlined in these recent important judgments from both the Supreme Court and Court of Appeal requires a move away from further procedure and timescales being introduced with legislative and policy changes. These currently simply support and reinforce a linear approach to decision making.

When the state is so concerned about the welfare of a child that it intends to seek an order to remove that child from their family, it is crucially important that decisions in respect of the most vulnerable children and their families are fair and proportionate (Herring, 2011). It is my view that the family justice system must provide the necessary safeguards in the most complex cases. Furthermore, if, as I contend, the court does appropriately take responsibility in the most complex cases, it must also accept that there are implications in taking on this responsibility in respect of increased resources and costs. Recent changes to private law proceedings introduced with the Legal Aid Sentencing and Punishment of Offenders Act (2012) have resulted in scenes within the family court that resemble a Dickensian novel with Pickwick delivering his papers, and litigants in person descending on the court with resulting chaos and confusion (Holt, 2013). Increasingly within private law proceedings we are witnessing the territory skirmishes that take place when alternative forms of dispute resolution are adopted in complex matters that require the oversight of the court.

There is overwhelming evidence that the courts are not appropriately resourced to manage the increased volume of work in family cases, but the government and the judiciary cannot simply reduce their timescales, leaving the most vulnerable children holding the risk whilst professionals try to navigate the administrative space. It is quite unacceptable that these important decisions are being ushered into a pre-proceedings protocol supporting the rhetoric of the timetable for the child. Let us be really clear that the rhetoric of the timetable for the child is a difficult one to dispute; but I strongly suggest that these changes are principally designed to reduce costs and court time. Achieving timely decision making with the 'timetable for the child' as the most important theme is indeed important. The timetable for the child within the context of a pre-proceedings protocol will at best remain the same, and at worst result in additional delay when diversion plans are not successful and important time has been wasted prior to an application being made (Holt, 2014a).

What Has Happened since the Family Justice Review

A Brighter Future for Children and their Families?

Three years after the Family Justice Review published its findings in November 2011, the Department for Education and the Ministry of Justice published *A Brighter Future for Family Justice* in November 2014 (DfE and MOJ, 2014). Following the publication of the *Family Justice Review: Final Report* (MOJ, 2011a) and *The Government Response to the Family Justice Review: A System with Children and Families at its Heart* (MOJ and DfE, 2012), there has been such a fundamental change, which has seen the abolition of legal aid, albeit for the exceptional cases, that the author is not persuaded that a brighter future is on the horizon, either for children and their families, or for a range of professionals working within the family justice system. Many in the legal profession have lost their jobs, and the social work profession is buckling under the pressure of yet further instrumental approaches to working with families, and additional targets and timeframes to be judged on (Holt and Kelly, 2014a). The Brighter Future report unsurprisingly refers to a system that was failing children and their families – highlighting mistrust between agencies and a lack of leadership.

There is no account in the report of the impact of the call centre or target-focused regimes in all areas of professional practice, but specifically within both the local authority (who have been affected by the inspection regime that removes professionals from the front line to a life behind the computer screen) and lawyers in private practice balancing the books (White, Morris and Featherstone, 2014).

Following the implementation of the Children and Families Act 2014, there has been a fundamental shift to move the majority of the business that the courts previously took responsibility for to a pre-proceedings space, whether this is within public law or private law proceedings. Indeed, the Ministry of Justice may be able to claim there has been a reduction in the duration of care proceedings from 60 weeks to an average of 32 weeks, but the problem has simply shifted elsewhere. This has resulted in increased levels of mistrust not only from within the judiciary but also from every other agency that is left carrying the burden of a pre-proceedings protocol without the additional resources to support this work and when these organizations are already overstretched (Holt and Kelly, 2014a).

The government agreed that radical action was needed to ensure the family justice system was operating effectively and efficiently, and accepted the recommendations of the review. Working towards a single Family Court and reducing costs generated excitement amongst senior members of the judiciary, who likened the change to something of a revolution. Elsewhere, the spillage from this revolution is being absorbed by agencies and organizations who are already overstretched and by parents who are denied access to justice with the abolition of both legal aid for the majority of family matters and access to legal help in some areas of the UK, where there are now advice deserts. Cases such as Re D (A Child), where the President found the absence of legal aid for the most vulnerable of parents to be 'profoundly disturbing', highlights the seriousness of the situation.

Furthermore, it was announced by the Ministry of Justice in July 2015 that 122 out of 460 courts will either close or relocate as part of the Ministry's economy drive that will save an estimated half a million pounds annually. Increased use of technology, including video, telephone and online conferencing, are being heralded as the vehicles for driving improvements. Given a recent announcement that public counters in courts are to be closed in an effort to assist and streamline customer services, the government's suggestion that court hearings could be transferred to council chambers or hotel rooms appears ill-conceived (MOJ, 2015).

These changes mark the second major court closures since 2010. The government have sought to reassure the public by stating that more than 95 per cent of citizens would be able to reach *their referred court* within an hour by car. In rural areas it is being proposed that the courts may relocate to other civic buildings (MOJ, 2015). The closure or relocation of nearly a quarter of the courts will have a profound impact on access to justice – even Charles Dickens would have struggled to arrive at court on time with his papers if he required a trip that would take an hour by car. In reality, most citizens who access the court don't have the privilege of owning a car or affording the journey to court, so the majority will walk to court. An hour's drive or the equivalent for the most vulnerable could translate to 60 miles – without a car, it could take several hours to navigate by public transport. It is further evidence of the government's intention to push ahead with reforms that will be irreversible, as there is clearly no appetite to support welfare.

The introduction of a single family court was heralded as both radical and revolutionary. In part, the single family court was born out of necessity given the proposed cuts to legal funding following the introduction of the Legal Aid Sentencing and Punishment of Offenders Act 2012. Notwithstanding the impact of further court closures, this has resulted in scenes in the family court, particularly in respect of private law matters, that resemble a Dickensian novel, as opposed to a revolutionary system of family justice in 2015 (Holt, 2013).

If the government is serious about the timetable for the child, then additional resources need to be made available to respond efficiently and effectively to reduce delays for the child, both at the pre-proceedings stage and following the making of a care and placement order.

Resources are not the only solution. Practice must move away from a remote control position, whereby the most experienced practitioners are adopting proportionate working practices that place a high value on recording rather than doing, towards a relationship-based approach that sees practitioners on the front line (Ferguson and Gates, 2013).

Morale amongst practitioners operating within this context has never been so low; in conversations with nearly 200 colleagues from both the legal and social work professions in the north-east there was unanimous confirmation that the cuts to legal aid have resulted in significant numbers of legal firms closing, and those who remain are concerned about the sustainability of their organization because of a lack of funding. Amongst social work professionals the pressures of work and the reporting and inspection requirements have intensified. The overwhelming view was that the revolution was nothing like the rhetoric being purported by the government, but rather widespread uncertainty, fear, blame and pressure and with little time for relationship-based practice.

Solicitors in private practice reported serious concerns regarding being unable to balance the books, and many firms were on the cusp of going out of business, with the resulting loss of knowledge, skills and expertise that were so highly regarded in the Family Justice Review but now threatened with being lost in the process. Local authority legal representatives and social work colleagues, including senior managers, were reporting an increased climate of regulation, instrumentalization and bureaucracy that has intensified rather than abated following the final report of Professor Eileen Munro. A release from the excessive burden of process in favour of autonomy and professional judgement was eagerly awaited, but unfortunately was not forthcoming (Munro, 2011).

A recent study commissioned by the Department for Education found that there are mixed experiences in the extent to which social workers are seen as experts in court, despite the need to raise the profile of the social work assessment in a context of austerity and with the reduction of expert evidence being allowed (DfE, 2015a).

The important issue is that despite the reform of family justice no agency or organization is reporting significant improvements in terms of outcomes for children and their families, nor could they identify improved relationships between the agencies themselves. There appears to be little hope, if any, of any change – this position has strengthened following the election of the current Conservative government, reinforcing almost immediately that tackling welfare was to be high on the political agenda (Holt and Kelly, 2015d). Reinforcing the dominant discourse of a less tolerant approach to welfare will only serve to be a further attack on the professionals who, in their chosen career, support the recipients of welfare, and attempt to improve the lives and experiences of those who have the most vulnerabilities (Byron, 2014).

The view from professionals working across the family justice system is that the shift away from relationship-based approaches to working with families is now so entrenched that many professionals don't have the institutional/organizational memory to recall a time where practitioners were able to undertake the volume of face-to-face work, or gain skill and confidence in relationship-based approaches, which will inevitably result in children and their families being prioritized (White, Morris and Featherstone, 2014). The priority for local authorities, and indeed all public services operating within an inspection culture, is on inputting data that provides an evidence trail, whereby organizations are able to demonstrate that they provide quality services that are good value for money, in anticipation of this information being reviewed and benchmarked against a standard (Featherstone *et al.*, 2014).

There was widespread professional mistrust of a system that awarded 'outstanding' ratings to agencies whose changes to practice had resulted in a shift away from face-to-face work in favour of cost cutting/proportionate working practices. At the same time there was recognition of how important achieving 'outstanding' is for a particular agency and, conversely, the serious consequences for failure (Jay, 2015).

Following the implementation of the Children and Families Act 2014, and the deadline of 26 weeks for the completion of the majority of cases, the same professionals who are operating within a highly regulated culture are having to respond yet further to highly prescribed procedures that leave no room for error and where performance against the target is a matter of public record. The introduction of the 26-week deadline for the completion of complex child care matters is arguably not an ambitious target when the professionals who are tasked with achieving this have become compliant to dictates, rules and procedures. Also, there is already a requirement within public law cases to attempt to divert cases, wherever possible and safe to do so, without the need to make an application to court; and where there is a need to do so, to attempt to narrow the issues the court needs to decide upon (Welbourne, 2014).

The reform of the family justice system, whilst recognizing the skill, knowledge and expertise of professionals working within the system, contains a subtext that local authorities have previously been making spurious applications to court without merit; this has never been my experience – quite the contrary. In too many cases there have been delays in making an application to court and the recent changes in the law may have only served to exacerbate this situation (Parton, 2014b).

It is concerning that the introduction of further instrumental approaches into a system which already adopts an incremental approach to child protection is not in the best interests of children. There is a culture and practice of professionals automatically moving families up to the next stage, from child in need, to child protection and then to pre-proceedings. These procedures, which operate concurrently rather than consecutively, can often leave professional fixed thinking unchallenged – as they often rely upon the same professionals operating under a different procedure, and in some circumstances, the involvement of the court at an earlier rather than later stage would challenge decision making and accelerate the outcomes for children (Holt, 2014a).

The 26-week deadline may support a rhetoric of the timetable for the child, but in reality it masks the overall timeframe for the child – who may, as a result of both the legislative changes and cuts to resources, be left waiting much longer in the most complex of cases without the independent oversight of the court at the earliest opportunity (Holt and Kelly, 2015d). Furthermore, Featherstone *et al.* (2014) raised concern that local authorities perceived the pre-proceedings protocol as *ticking a box*, particularly in long-term neglect cases where the local authority had increasing concern, but where there was no one particular incident that could justify an emergency application, and the local authority had exhausted all available options.

The challenges for practice continue, following the high-profile serious case reviews in Rotherham and Oxfordshire, whereby local Safeguarding Children's Board processes and practices were in the public spotlight and government ministers were openly critical of professional practice that was identified as leaving hundreds of children exposed to sexual exploitation. Notwithstanding the complexities around child sexual exploitation, as is highlighted in Chapter 6, ministerial criticism and the media coverage have done nothing to improve morale amongst a range of professionals. In one policy document they are heralded as being key to improving the lives of the most vulnerable children and simultaneously blamed for failing to deal effectively with complex systemic child sexual abuse when these same professionals have seen relationship-based approaches to working with children eroded, which is crucially important in the recognition and response to child abuse (Jordan and Drakeford, 2012).

The role of the Children and Family Court Advisory and Support Service (Cafcass) has been pivotal in supporting the changes implemented by the Children and Families Act 2014, in terms of both public law and private law cases. Historically, the role of the family court advisor was relied upon to provide an independent voice and assessment for the child, and to advise the court from an independent position but with the expertise and time permitted to engage in this complex work. The family court advisor has also experienced the introduction of proportionate working practices that have eroded the time available for the relationship-based approaches to working with children, their families, relatives, carers and other professionals that have been central to their work.

It is clear from the 'outstanding' rating that proportionate working practices and a removal of relationship-based approaches to working with families, even in the most complex of cases, is being rewarded. This confirms practitioner narratives from all organizations/agencies operating within the family justice system that a remote control approach in a climate of severe cuts to welfare is the most cost-effective way. But we must remember that both care costs and the protection of children are being sacrificed within a climate of cuts to resources that are crucial to the welfare of children and their families who turn to a system when they are in crisis and unable to resolve their difficulties without professional support.

Furthermore, Doward and Sloggett (2015) reported on the anguish for children and their families following the closure of family contact centres. These centres are pivotal for separated parents who cannot agree contact arrangements. The National Association for Child Contact Centres (NACCC) confirmed that 40 centres have closed since the introduction of the Legal Aid, Sentencing and Punishment of Offenders Act 2012 came into force in 2013, and further closures are anticipated. Following the removal of legal aid to parents, the number of referrals to the centres has nearly halved, from 15,000 in 2013 to 9000 in 2014, and referrals from solicitors halved during the same period. NACCC believe parents simply do not know who to contact for help; usually their first point of contact would be a solicitor who would make the service known to parents, but this is no longer available. The closure of nearly 10 per cent of the centres has directly impacted on children, parents and grandparents, as there are parts of the UK with no centres available at all.

The closure of contact centres will have a disproportionate impact on fathers, who in nine out of ten cases are the non-resident parent and for whom the contact centre is vital in terms of maintaining relationships with their children in a neutral space (Doward and Sloggett, 2015).

The impact of changes introduced with the Family Justice Review arguably could not have been fully anticipated. The interface between public law and private law is one such area. It appears almost inconceivable that a parent without legal advice and representation should face defending themselves against both the local authority, which has intervened in the proceedings and is represented, and the other parent who is also represented (*Re D (Non-Availability of Legal Aid)* [2014]). Professionals operating within the family justice system are tasked with working with individuals with the most profound vulnerabilities, and it requires skill, knowledge and expertise to navigate these complexities, within a changing landscape for family justice that has directly impacted the recipients of welfare, as in the case of *Re D*. It has also had an impact on those professionals working within this context, with the closure of legal firms and resulting loss of jobs, and judicial criticism when professionals are not compliant with the protocols and targets, notwithstanding the stress of operating within a climate of severe cuts to public spending (Byron, 2014).

During 2014, there was a plethora of judgments from the Supreme Court, Court of Appeal and the High Court, notably: *Re B (A Child) (Care Proceedings: Threshold Criteria)* [2013]; *Re B-S (Children)* [2013]; *Re A and B v Rotherham Metropolitan Borough Council* [2014]; *Re J and S (Children)* [2014]; *Re C (A Child)* [2013]; and *Re R (A Child)* [2014]. These have resulted in widespread uncertainty amongst professionals, and potential conflict between both professionals and parents when judicial decisions appear to have opened the floodgates for appeals to care and placement orders. Regardless of the intention, these cases will inevitably impact on both decision making within the local authority (who are understandably influenced by judicial comments) and delay in respect of securing the best outcomes for children.

The President attempted to allay concerns when he delivered his judgment in *Re R*:

> I wish to emphasise, with as much force as possible, that Re B-S was not intended to change and has not changed the law. Where adoption is in the child's best interests, local authorities must not shy away from seeking, nor courts from making, care orders with a plan for adoption, placement orders and adoption orders. The fact is that there are occasions when nothing but adoption will do, and it is essential in such cases that a child's welfare should not be compromised by keeping them within their family at all costs. (*Re R (A Child)* [2014] EWCA Civ 1625 16 December 2014 [44])

The issue of detailed assessment and planning shows no sign of abating, with the President taking the opportunity in *Re A* [2015] to highlight a lack of analysis in assessments on the part of both the local authority and Cafcass. There is a concern that in a climate of error and blame, with proportionate working practices and with social workers and family court advisors spending less time on relationship-based approaches with children and their families, they face being placed between a rock and a hard place. They are torn between the need to maintain the target-driven key performance indicators that reward 'outstanding', or the aspirations of the court to achieve holistic assessments, when key professionals are increasingly reliant upon second- and third-hand information that is shoehorned into an assessment form.

The situation is untenable, and despite attempts to introduce innovative projects that seek to mobilize resources to working with families before the case escalates, these measures always appear short-lived, especially within a climate of severe cuts to public funding and an inspection culture that requires compliance.

Furthermore, where innovation within the family justice system has been successful it has highlighted how good multi-agency working can improve outcomes for children and their families. The Family Drug and Alcohol Court (FDAC) provided an innovative approach to care proceedings, where parental substance misuse was a key component of the local authority's concern that had informed the decision to commence care proceedings. The FDAC approach is a court-based family intervention that attempts to address parental difficulties within the context of court proceedings, which for some parents will provide a clear lever for change. Essentially the model is designed to identify the issues and find solutions that will result in either lifestyle changes which enable children to be reunited with their parents or, where this is not safe to do so, finding permanent placements for children – ensuring that delay for children is kept to a minimum.

The success of the FDAC model within Inner London has stimulated interest from other areas. The strengths of this model are achieving a holistic assessment of the family and thereby avoiding delay in achieving permanent outcomes for children (Harwin *et al.*, 2014).

Importantly, the emphasis must be on achieving sustainable outcomes for children and their families. Whilst the emphasis within this book has been on achieving diversion from court, wherever it is possible and safe to do so, there is little benefit to a child if diversionary strategies result in a revolving-door approach to care, and cases are returned to court, as there has not been the time or resources deployed to ensure either a return to parents or a placement for permanency being sustainable (Holt, 2014a).

Successive government policies have made it abundantly clear that individuals should attempt to resolve their disputes outside of the courts, wherever possible, and in many instances this was achieved prior to any legislative change; avoiding costs, additional acrimony and judicial scrutiny when a situation is already stressful is what most reasonable individuals seek. However, there are situations when resolving a dispute amicably and without the oversight of the court is simply not desirable or achievable, and in these circumstances there should be a right to legal aid and legal representation. Applying a blanket rule that legal aid will only be available for mediation, and introducing a statutory requirement for all separating couples to consider mediation before they can proceed to court over financial and child care matters, are creating further procedure in a process that is already complicated for individuals and may result in situations that are wholly unjust (see *Re H* [2014]).

The measure of success within the family justice system, where children and their families are at the heart of the system, must be to resolve disputes, whether in public or private law cases, in a manner that is sustainable and not simply driven by a desire to reduce costs in one area of the system, which will inevitably result in spillage elsewhere in the system.

Glossary

Accommodated child   Parents may agree to their child being accommodated or looked after by the local authority under section 20 of the Children Act 1989, whilst an investigation and/or an assessment is undertaken. The local authority will not have parental responsibility for the child if they are accommodated this way; the parents retain full and exclusive parental responsibility. The local authority has a duty to let the parents know where the child is and maintain contact between the child and the parent.

If the young person is 16 or 17 years old, they do not need the consent of those with parental responsibility in order to be accommodated by the local authority.

A local authority may also provide accommodation to anyone between 16 and 21 years if they consider it necessary to safeguard or promote that young person's welfare.

Under section 31 of the Children Act 1989, the local authority or any authorized person can apply to the court for a child or young person to become the subject of a care order. The local authority may also accommodate a child who is the subject of a care order.

Alternative dispute resolution   Refers to any means of settling disputes between the relevant individuals outside of the courtroom.

Care order   Under section 31 of the Children Act 1989, the local authority or any authorized person can apply to the court for a child or young person to become the subject of a care order.

The court will only make a care order if it believes that it is better for the child or young person than not making an order.

Once a care order is made, the local authority obtains parental responsibility in addition to the other parental responsibility holders.

A care order can only be discharged by the court on the application of any person who has parental responsibility for the child or the local authority designated by the order.

Care proceedings   The local authority can initiate care proceedings if they are concerned about a child's welfare, and the local authority consider the threshold criteria for making an application to court can be evidenced to the court.

Section 31 of the Children Act 1989 sets out the legal basis or the 'threshold criteria' on which a Family Court can make a care or supervision order to a designated local authority in respect of a particular child. This is: that the child must be suffering, or likely to suffer, significant harm; and that the harm or likelihood of harm must be attributable to one of the following:

    a) the care given to the child, or likely to be given if the order were not made, not being what it would be reasonable to expect a parent to give; or

    b) the child being beyond parental control.

The local authority can apply for a care order which will allow the local authority to share parental responsibility with the parent who holds parental responsibility, but it is the local authority who has the power to decide important decisions about the child, including where the child should live.

Child in need   Section 17 of the Children Act 1989 defines a child as being in need if:

> He or she is unlikely to achieve or maintain or to have the opportunity to achieve or maintain a reasonable standard of health or development without provision of services from the local authority.

> His or her health or development is likely to be significantly impaired, or further impaired, without the provision of services from the local authority.

> He or she has a disability.

'Development' can mean physical, intellectual, emotional, social or behavioural development. 'Health' can be physical or mental health.

The local authority may provide accommodation under section 20 of the Children Act 1989 to a child who is in need and is required to be living away from his or her family.

The local authority is under a duty to safeguard and promote the welfare of children who are in need and living in their area, and to provide services/resources to promote a child continuing to live with their own family, where it is safe to do so.

The local authority must assess a child in need and their family; the guidance used is the DoH's Framework for the Assessment of Children in Need and their Families (2000). The use of this guidance will enable professionals working with the child and their family to undertake a detailed assessment, including a risk assessment, that will inform what resources and services are required to promote the child's welfare.

Child protection plan   A plan that is agreed and formulated at the initial child protection conference, which should outline in detail how the child is to be kept safe, how their health and development is to be promoted and the level of support required by professionals to assist the child's family in promoting the child's welfare.

Following the initial child protection conference, relevant professionals together with parents/carers will further develop the plan. If the child is accommodated by the local authority the child protection plan should form part of the child's care plan (for further information see *Working Together*, DfE, 2015b).

Family court advisor   Following the implementation of the Children and Families Act 2014, the court can take up to 26 weeks to make a decision in respect of the child. Some complex cases may take longer than this, but these will be very exceptional cases.

During this time a social worker, an officer from the Children and Family Court Advisory and Support Service (Cafcass) and other professionals will be assessing the reasons why the child may be at risk. In order to complete a detailed assessment they will talk to the parents, the child, extended family members and relevant professionals who know the family. The family court advisor will prepare a report for the court and this report will outline what they consider to be the best outcome for the child.

Financial dispute resolution (FDR)   The financial dispute resolution (FDR) appointment was introduced into the court process on a trial basis in 1996, and was formally incorporated in the revised rules governing financial ancillary relief cases in June 2000. It was an innovative development, designed to enable the parties, with the assistance of the judge, to identify and seek to resolve the real issues in the case, at a time and in a manner intended to limit the overall financial cost for the parties, to reduce delay in resolving the case and to lessen the emotional and practical strain on the family of continuing litigation.

Over ten years on, the procedure continues to provide a timely and effective means of resolving many financial disputes. A recent trend has seen a rise in private FDRs as an alternative to court-based hearings. Mediation has also become an attractive alternative for many parties. The introduction of the Family Procedure Rules 2010 (as from 6 April 2011) has again focused attention on the process for financial cases, with the extension of the standard process beyond matrimonial and civil partnership cases, to include proceedings for financial provision for children under the Children Act 1989, Schedule 1 and certain other financial applications (collectively termed 'financial remedy' applications).

(For further information see *Financial Dispute Resolution Appointments*, FJC, 2012.)

Guardian (guardian ad litem) (GAL)   The guardian ad litem service was first identified in England in 1973 following the death of a child, Maria Colwell.

One of the recommendations following the tragic death of Maria Colwell was the requirement of an independent social work report to assist the court in determining the best outcome for the child in care proceedings.

In 1989 the introduction of the Children Act expanded and enhanced the role of guardian ad litem (GAL), making it possible to appoint a GAL in all specified proceedings and retain the role of the GAL in adoption proceedings.

The role of the GAL is to represent the child before the court on what is in the child's best interests and to ensure that the child's wishes and feelings are made clear to the court.

GALs are qualified social workers who are expected to have considerable experience of complex child care matters and a detailed understanding of family law.

Independent reviewing officer (IRO)   Independent reviewing officers (IROs) were introduced with the Adoption and Children Act 2002, section 118. The intention of the change to legislation was to introduce independent scrutiny of local authority care plans for all children who are in the care of the local authority.

The role of the IRO is therefore to promote the welfare of the child, which involves listening to the child and others about the plan; the IRO must be able to challenge the local authority if they are of the view that the plan is not in the best interests of the child.

Letter before proceedings   The Public Law Outline (PLO) (MOJ, 2008) replaced the Protocol for Judicial Case Management (2003) in England and Wales, and required a reordering of the way care proceedings are instigated, structured and conducted. The PLO involves two stages: 'pre-proceedings' and 'post instigation of proceedings'. In the pre-proceedings stage the aim is to maximize the possibility of resolving cases without proceedings, making mandatory certain steps that are to be taken prior to proceedings being issued.

Should the local authority consider that proceedings are necessary (and not of such a nature that the welfare of the child requires immediate court protection) they must convene a meeting between the social worker and local authority legal advisor (a legal planning meeting), and a letter before proceedings must be sent to parents. This letter must summarize concerns, state actions required to remedy those concerns, provide information on what the local authority has done to safeguard the children to date and state what outcome would be likely if the concerns are not addressed. The letter before proceedings invites parents to a pre-proceedings meeting to be convened with the local authority legal advisor and social worker/s, and must advise parents on how to obtain legal advice and representation at that meeting.

Looked-after child   Parents may agree to their child being 'looked after' by the local authority under section 20 of the Children Act 1989, while an investigation and/or an assessment is undertaken.

McKenzie friend   A McKenzie friend is a person who accompanies a litigant in person to a court hearing for the purpose of assisting them at court, for example, taking notes, helping the litigant in person to navigate the documents, and generally offering support and suggestions that may involve how to put questions to a witness. Although usually a non-lawyer, the McKenzie friend should not be thought of as a lay advocate, and they have no right to address the court.

Mediation Information and Assessment Meeting (MIAM)   The MIAM is a meeting between one or both individuals who are intending to separate and a mediator, to establish whether there are alternative solutions to any dispute that may avoid having to go to court.

The mediator will explain the options available, the role of mediation, the benefits of mediation and other forms of dispute resolution and the costs, if any, of using mediation.

The meeting can be arranged with one or both individuals, and usually lasts around one hour.

The mediator will decide if the case is suitable for mediation, and advise on the next stages of the procedure. If the mediator considers that mediation is not suitable, the mediator will provide signed documentation to this effect, and confirm attendance at a MIAM. A court will then allow an application to issue proceedings.

Placement order   A Placement Order, made under section 21 of the Adoption and Children Act 2002, gives a local authority the legal right to place a child with prospective adopters. It can only be made in relation to a child who is the subject of a care order or where the threshold criteria for a care order are satisfied or where there is no parent or guardian.

Parental consent to the placement order may be dispensed with by the court under section 47 of the Adoption and Children Act 2002 on the grounds that:

The parent cannot be found or is incapable of giving consent.

Or the welfare of the child requires the consent to be dispensed with.

A placement order has the effect of suspending a care order. If the placement order is subsequently revoked, the care order is reinstated.

The placement order continues until it is revoked or until an adoption order is made or until the child is 18, marries or enters a civil partnership.

Only a local authority can apply for a placement order and such an order is required before a child can be placed for adoption with prospective adoptive parents unless parental consent to the placement has been given to the placement.

Prospective adopters will acquire parental responsibility for the child as soon as the child is placed with them, to be shared with the birth parents and the adoption agency making the placement.

Pre-proceedings meeting (*see* letter before proceedings)   The aim of the meeting is to agree a plan for the child (which should be in writing), and be clear what needs to be done, by whom and timescales, to avoid the local authority making an application to court for a care order.

It should be very clear what is expected of everyone and the timescales for carrying out the plan. This plan needs to be reviewed within six weeks to assess how the plan is progressing, and ensure that the welfare of the child remains central to the plan. If the plan is not effective in reducing risk for the child, the local authority will have to consider making an application to court.

Pre-proceedings stage (*see* letter before proceedings, pre-proceedings meeting) The pre-proceedings stage is what happens when the local authority have concerns about the welfare of a child and are considering applying for a care order. This is now a formal process that the local authority are required to follow.

The Public Law Outline (2008) introduced a formal pre-proceedings protocol. There have been subsequent revisions with the Public Law Outline: Guide to Case Management in Public Law Proceedings, which came into effect on 6 April 2010; followed by further revision on 22 April 2014; alongside the statutory 26-week time-limit for completion of care and supervision proceedings under the Children and Families Act 2014.

The Public Law Outline sets out streamlined case management procedures for dealing with public law children's cases. The intention is to identify and focus on the key issues for the child, with the aim of making the best decisions for them within the timetable set by the court, and avoiding the need for unnecessary evidence or hearings.

The pre-proceedings stage enables cases to be managed in a structured way, leading to a decision about whether or not to divert the case away from proceedings by resolving the issues and reducing risk to the child or placing them with family members; where the risk for the child is assessed as being too high the local authority may issue proceedings.

Pro bono Legal advice or representation provided by lawyers to individuals and community groups who cannot afford to pay for that advice or representation and where public funding is not available.

Protected child A protected child is a child who has not been placed for adoption by an agency. Instead the local authorities are involved in ensuring that the child's interests are protected in the adoption proceedings.

Supervision order The court can make a supervision order to a local authority if it considers that the threshold criteria under section 31(2) of the Children Act 1989 have been met; that it is in the child's best interests to do so; and that it considers it necessary and proportionate to make such an order.

A supervision order places the child under the supervision of the local authority. The local authority has three duties towards the child under the supervision order:

to advise, befriend and assist the child;

to take steps that are necessary to give the order full effect;

if the order is not followed, or the supervisor feels that the order is no longer needed, to consider whether to vary the order, attach requirements to it or even substitute it for a care order.

Case References

Re A [2015] EWFC 11

Re A and B v Rotherham Metropolitan Borough Council [2014] EWFC 47

Re B (Care: Interference with Family Life) [2003] EWCA Civ 786 [2003] 2 FLR 813

Re B (A Child) [2013] UKSC 22

Re B (A Child) (Care Proceedings: Threshold Criteria) [2013] UKSC 33

Re B-S (Children) [2013] EWCA Civ 1146

Re C (A Child) [2013] EWCA Civ 431

Re D (Abduction: Rights of Custody) [2006] UKHL 51

Re D (Non-Availability of Legal Aid) [2014] EWFC 39 [2015] 1 FLR

Re D (A Child) (No 1) [2014] EWFC 39

Re D (A Child) (No 2) [2015] EWFC 2

Re E (A Child) [2014] EWHC 6 (Fam)

Re G (A Child) [2013] EWCA Civ 965

Re H [2014] EWFC B127

Re J and S (Children) [2014] EWFC 4

Re KD (A Minor) (Ward: Termination of Access) [1988] 1 AC 806 [1988] 2 FLR 139

Re K-H (Children) [2015] EWCA Civ 543

Re K and H (Children: Unrepresented Father: Cross-Examination of Child) [2015] EWFC 1

Re P (Adoption: Leave Provisions) [2007] EWCA Civ 616 [2007] 2 FLR 1069

Re P (A Child) [2013] EWCA Civ 963

Re R (A Child) [2014] EWCA Civ 1625 (16 December 2014)

Re S (Minors) (Care Order: Implementation of Care Plan); Re W (Minors) (Care Order: Adequacy of Care Plan) [2002] UKHL 10 [2002] 1 FLR 815

Re S [2004] WL 62115

Re S, K v The London Borough of Brent [2013] EWCA Civ 926

Re V (Children) [2013] EWCA Civ 913

Re W and B; Re W (Care Plan) [2001] EWCA Civ 757 [2001] 2 FLR 582

AD and OD v United Kingdom (Application No 28680/06) (16 March 2010)

H v W [2013] EWHC 4105 (Fam)

H v W [2014] EWHC 2846 (Fam)

Mann v Mann [2014] EWHC 537 (Fam)

P, C and S v United Kingdom [2002] 2 FLR 631

Q v Q; Re B (A Child); Re C (A Child) [2014] EWFC 31

R (L and Others) v Manchester City Council [2001] EWHC 707 (Admin), [2002] 1 FLR 43, 8 CCLR 268
RP and Others v United Kingdom (Application No 38245/08) [2013] 1 FLR 744
S v Rochdale [2008] EWHC 3283 (Fam)
W v W [2010] EWHC 332 (Fam)
YC v United Kingdom (Application No 4547/10) [2012] 2 FLR 332

References

Aldgate, J. (1991) 'Attachment Theory and its Application to Child Care Social Work – An Introduction.' In J. Lishman (ed.) *Handbook of Theory for Practice Teachers in Social Work.* London: Jessica Kingsley Publishers.

Aldgate, J. and Simmonds, J. (eds) (1988) *Direct Work with Children: A Guide for Social Work Practitioners.* London: Batsford.

Baksi, C., Rayner, J., Cross, M. and Hyde, J. (2014) 'Bid to save legal aid for domestic violence victims.' [online] *Law Society Gazette.*

Bar Council (2012) *Bar Council and FLBA Urge Care on Family Justice Reforms.* London: Bar Council.

Bar Council (2014a) *New Legal Aid Figures Show the Depth of Legal Aid Cuts.* London: Bar Council.

Bar Council (2014b) *The Legal Aid, Sentencing and Punishment of Offenders Act 2012 (LASPO): One Year On: Final Report.* London: Bar Council.

Barlow, A., Hunter, R., Smithson, J. and Ewing, J. (2014) *Mapping Paths to Family Justice. ESRC Funded Interdisciplinary Project.* Exeter: University of Exeter.

Bazeley, P. (2013) *Qualitative Data Analysis: Practical Strategies.* London: Sage.

Booth, M. (1996) *Avoiding Delay in Children Act Cases.* London: LCD.

Brandon, M., Bailey, S., Belderson, P., Gardner, R. *et al.* (2009) *Understanding Serious Case Reviews and their impact: A biennial analysis of serious case reviews 2005–2007.* Research Report DCSF RR129. London: Department for Children, Schools and Families.

Brandon, M., Sidebotham, P., Bailey, S., Belderson, P., Hawley, C., Ellis, C. and Megson, M. (2012) *New Learning from Serious Case Reviews: A Two Year Report for 2009–2011.* Research Report DFE-RR226. Norwich: Centre for Research on the Child and Family, University of East Anglia, and Coventry: Health Sciences Research Institute, University of Warwick.

Brandon, M., Sidebothom, P., Ellis, C., Bailey, S. and Belderson, P. (2011) *Child and Family Practitioners' Understanding of Child Development: Lessons learnt from a small sample of serious case reviews.* London: Department for Education.

Braun, V. and Clarke, V. (2006) 'Using thematic analysis in psychology.' *Qualitative Research in Psychology 3,* 2, 77–101.

Broadhurst, K. (2009) 'Safeguarding Children through Parenting Support: How Does Every Parent Matter?' In K. Broadhurst, C. Grover and J. Jamieson (eds) *Critical Perspectives on Safeguarding Children.* Oxford: Wiley-Blackwell.

Broadhurst, K. and Holt, K.E. (2010) 'Partnership and the limits of procedure: Prospects for relationships between parents and professionals under the new Public Law Outline.' *Child and Family Social Work 15*, 1, 97–106.

Broadhurst, K. and Holt, K.E. (2012) 'Involving the Family Court Advisor in pre-proceedings practice: Initial lessons from the Coventry and Warwickshire Pilot.' *Family Law Week*, 17 April 2012.

Broadhurst, K. and Mason, C. (2013) 'Maternal outcasts: Raising the profile of women who are vulnerable to successive, compulsory removals of their children – a plea for preventative action.' *Journal of Social Welfare & Family Law 35*, 3, 291–304.

Broadhurst, K. and May-Chahal, C. (2006) 'Integrating objects of intervention and organizational relevance: The case of safeguarding children missing from education systems.' *Child Abuse Review 15*, 6, 440–455.

Broadhurst, K., Grover, C. and Jamieson, J. (2009) 'Conclusion.' In K. Broadhurst, C. Grover and J. Jamieson (eds) *Critical Perspectives on Safeguarding Children*. Oxford: Wiley-Blackwell.

Broadhurst, K., Holt, K.E. and Doherty, P. (2011) 'Accomplishing parental engagement in child protection practice? A qualitative analysis of parent–professional interaction in pre-proceedings work under the Public Law Outline.' *Qualitative Social Work 11*, 5, 517–534.

Broadhurst, K., Holt, K.E., Kelly, N. and Doherty, P. (2012) *Coventry and Warwickshire Pre-proceedings Pilot: Interim Report*. London: Cafcass.

Broadhurst, K., Holt, K., Kelly, N. and Doherty, P. (2013) *Coventry and Warwickshire Pre-proceedings Pilot. Final Report*. London: Cafcass.

Brophy, J. (2006) *Research Review: Child Care Proceedings under the Children Act 1989*. DCA Research Series 5/06. London: MOJ.

Brown, R. and Ward, H. (2013) *Decision Making within a Child's Timeframe: An Overview of Current Research for Family Justice Professionals Concerning Child Development and the Impact of Maltreatment*. Loughborough: Childhood Wellbeing Research Centre, Loughborough University.

Buchanan, A. (1994) *Partnership in Practice: The Children Act 1989*. Avebury: Ashgate.

Buckley, H. (2009) 'Reforming the child protection system: Why we need to be careful what we wish for.' *Irish Journal of Family Law 12*, 2, 27–31.

Byron, J. (2014) 'Unintended consequences of family justice reform.' *Family Law Week*, 27 June 2014.

CAADA (2014) *In Plain Sight: The Evidence from Children Exposed to Domestic Abuse*. Research Report. Bristol: CAADA. Available at www.safelives.org.uk/sites/default/files/resources/In_plain_sight_the_evidence_from_children_exposed_to_domestic_abuse.pdf, accessed on 19 December 2015.

Castell, S. (2007) *Understanding Attitudes to Poverty in the UK: Getting the Public's Attention*. York: Joseph Rowntree Foundation. Available at http://www.jrf.org.uk/report/understanding-attitudes-poverty-uk-getting-publics-attention, accessed on 15 March 2016.

Chakrabati, S. (2014) *Liberty*. London: Penguin.

Cicchetti, D. and Valentino, K. (2006) 'An Ecological Transactional Perspective on Child Maltreatment: Failure of the Average Expectable Environment and its Influence upon Child Development.' In D. Cicchetti and D.J. Cohen (eds) *Developmental Psychopathology* (2nd edn) *Vol. 3: Risk, Disorder, and Adaptation.* New York, NY: Wiley.

Cleaver, H., Unell, I. and Aldgate, J. (1999) *Children's Needs – Parenting Capacity: The Impact of Parental Mental Illness, Problem Alcohol and Drug Use, and Domestic Violence on Children's Development.* London: TSO.

Corby, B., Miller, M. and Young, L. (1996) 'Parental participation in child protection work: Rethinking the rhetoric.' *British Journal of Social Work 26*, 4, 475–492.

Daniel, B., Burgess, C. and Scott, J. (2012) *Review of Child Neglect in Scotland.* Edinburgh: Scottish Government.

Daniel, B., Taylor, J. and Scott, J. (2011) *Recognising and Helping the Neglected Child: Evidence Based Practice for Assessment and Intervention.* London: Jessica Kingsley Publishers.

Department for Constitutional Affairs (2006a) *Review of Childcare Proceedings in England and Wales.* London: DCA.

Department for Constitutional Affairs (2006b) *Legal Aid – A Market-Based Approach to Reform (Lord Carter's Review of Legal Aid Procurement).* London: DCA.

Department for Constitutional Affairs (2008) *A Fairer Deal for Legal Aid.* Cm 6591. London: TSO.

Department for Education (2013) *Characteristics of Children in Need in England, 2012–13: Statistical First Release.* London: DfE.

Department for Education (2013–2015) *Statistics: Looked-After Children.* London: DfE. Available at www.gov.uk/government/collections/statistics-looked-after-children, accessed on 15 March 2016.

Department for Education (2014a) *Children in Care and Adoption Performance Tables 2013.* Available at www.gov.uk/government/publications/children-in-care-and-adoption-performance-tables-2013, accessed on 19 December 2015.

Department for Education (2014b) *Court Orders and Pre-proceedings for Local Authorities.* London: DfE.

Department for Education (2015a) *Impact of the Family Justice Reforms on Front-line Practice Phase One: The Public Law Outline. Research Report.* London: DfE.

Department for Education (2015b) *Working Together to Safeguard Children.* Available at www.gov.uk/government/publications/working-together-to-safeguard-children--2. London: DfE, accessed on 15 March 2016.

Department for Education (2015c) *Transparency Data: Adoption Leadership Board Quarterly Data Reports: 2014 to 2015.* London: DfE.

Department for Education (2015d) *Child Death Reviews: Year Ending 31 March 2015.* London: DfE.

Department for Education (2015e) *Characteristics of Children in Need.* London: DfE.

Department for Education (2015f) *Children Looked After in England, Including Adoption: 2014 to 2015.* London: DfE.

Department for Education and Ministry of Justice (2014) *A Brighter Future for Family Justice.* London: DfE/MOJ.

Department for Education and Skills (2005) *Parental Separation: Children's Needs and Parents' Responsibilities.* London: HMSO.

Department of Health (1995) *Child Protection: Messages from Research.* London: HMSO.

Department of Health (2000) *Framework for the Assessment of Children in Need and their Families.* London: TSO.

Dickens, J. (2006) 'Care, control and change in child care proceedings: Dilemmas for social workers, managers and lawyers.' *Child and Family Social Work 11,* 1, 23–32.

Dickens, J. (2012) *Social Work, Law and Ethics.* Oxford: Routledge.

Doughty, J. (2013) 'Re B (A Child) [2013] UKSC 33.' *Journal of Social Welfare and Family Law 35,* 4, 491–501.

Doward, J. and Sloggett, C. (2015) 'Legal aid cuts hit divided families as Contact Centres close down.' *The Guardian,* 17 January 2015.

Drew, P. and Heritage, J. (eds) (1992) *Talk at Work.* Cambridge: Cambridge University Press.

Dumbrill, G.C. (2006) 'Parental experience of child protection intervention: A qualitative study.' *Child Abuse and Neglect 30,* 1, 27–37.

Eastman, A. (2014) *Enough is Enough: A Report on Child Protection and Mental Health Services for Children and Young People.* London: Centre for Social Justice.

Economic and Social Research Council (2010) *ESRC Framework for Research Ethics (FRE) 2010.* Updated September 2012. Swindon: ESRC.

Fahlberg, V.I. (1981) *Attachment and Separation.* London: BAAF.

Fahlberg, V.I. (1991) *A Child's Journey through Placement.* London: BAAF.

Family Group Unions Parliamentary Group (2014) *The Impact of Legal Aid Cuts on Family Justice.* London: NAPO, SM, PCS.

Family Justice Council (2012) *Financial Dispute Resolution Appointments: Best Practice Guidance.* London: FJC. Available at www.judiciary.gov.uk/wp content/uploads/2014/10/fjc_financial_dispute_resolution.pdf, accessed on 1 April 2016.

Featherstone, B. and Broadhurst, K. (2003) 'Engaging parents and carers with family support services: What can be learned from research on help-seeking?' *Child and Family Social Work 8,* 4, 341–350.

Featherstone, B., Broadhurst, K. and Holt, K. (2012) 'Thinking systemically – thinking politically: Building strong partnerships with children and families in the context of rising inequality.' *British Journal of Social Work 42,* 4, 618–633.

Featherstone, B., Fraser, C., Ashley, C. and Ledward, P. (2011) 'Advocacy for parents and carers involved with children's services: Making a difference to working in partnership?' *Child and Family Social Work 16,* 3, 266–275.

Featherstone, B., Hooper, C.A., Scourfield, J. and Taylor, J. (eds) (2010) *Gender and Child Welfare in Society.* Chichester: Wiley.

Featherstone, B., Morris, K. and White, S. (2014) 'A marriage made in hell: Early intervention meets child protection.' *British Journal of Social Work 44*, 7, 1735–1749.

Ferguson, H. (2004) *Protecting Children in Time: Child Abuse, Child Protection and the Consequences of Modernity.* Basingstoke: Palgrave Macmillan.

Ferguson, H. (2009) 'Performing child protection: Home visiting, movement and the struggle to reach the abused child.' *Child and Family Social Work 14*, 4, 471–480.

Ferguson, H. (2010a) 'Therapeutic journeys: The car as a vehicle for working with children and families and theorising practice.' *Journal of Social Work Practice 24*, 2, 121–138.

Ferguson, H. (2010b) 'Walks, home visits and atmospheres: Risk and the everyday practices and mobilities of social work and child protection.' *British Journal of Social Work 40*, 4, 1100–1117.

Ferguson, H. (2011) *Child Protection Practice.* Basingstoke: Palgrave Macmillan.

Ferguson, H. and Gates, P. (2013) 'Early intervention and holistic, relationship-based practice with fathers: Evidence from the work of the Family Nurse Partnership.' *Child and Family Social Work 20*, 1, 96–105.

Fish, S., Munro, E. and Bairstow, S. (2008) *Learning Together to Safeguard Children: Developing a Multi-agency Systems Approach for Case Reviews.* London: Social Care Institute for Excellence.

Forrester, D. (2013) *Final Report of a Comparative Study of Practice and the Factors Shaping it in Three Local Authorities.* Luton: Tilda Goldberg Centre for Social Work and Social Care, University of Bedfordshire.

Forrester, D., Kershaw, S., Moss, H. and Hughes, L. (2008) 'Communication skills in child protection: How do social workers talk to parents?' *Child and Family Social Work 13*, 1, 41–51.

Fortin, J. (2009) *Children's Rights and the Developing Law* (3rd edn) *Law in Context.* New York, NY: Cambridge University Press.

Freeman, P. and Hunt, J. (1998) *Parental Perspectives on Care Proceedings.* London: TSO.

Frost, N. and Parton, N. (2009) *Understanding Children's Social Care: Politics, Policy and Practice.* London: Sage.

Ghate, D. and Ramella , M. (2002) *Positive Parenting: The National Evaluation of the Youth Justice Board's Parenting Programme.* London: Policy Research Bureau for the Youth Justice Board.

Gibbons, J., Gallagher, B., Bell, C. and Gordon, D. (1995) *Development after Physical Abuse in Early Childhood.* London: HMSO.

Giddens, A. (1998) *The Third Way: The Renewal of Social Democracy.* Cambridge: Polity.

Gillies, V. (2005) 'Meeting parents' needs? Discourses of "support" and "inclusion" in family policy.' *Critical Social Policy 25*, 1, 70–90.

Gilligan, P., Manby, M. and Pickburn, C. (2011) 'Fathers' involvement in children's services: Exploring local and national issues in "Moorlandstown".' *British Journal of Social Work 42*, 3, 500–518.

Goffman, E. (1983) 'The interaction order.' *American Sociological Review 48*, 1, 1–17.

Grover, C. (2008) *Crime and Inequality.* Cullompton: Willan.

Gupta, A. and Lloyd-Jones, E. (2014) 'Re B-S: A glass half full? An exploration of the implications of the Re B-S judgment on practice in the family courts.' *Child and Family Social Work.* DOI: 10.1111/cfs.12176.

Harlow, E. and Shardlow, S. (2006) 'Safeguarding children: Challenges to the effective operation of core groups.' *Child and Family Social Work 11*, 1, 65–72.

Harwin, J., Broadhurst, K., Kershaw, S., Shaw, M., Alrouh, B. and Mason, C. (2014) 'Recurrent care proceedings: Part 2: Young motherhood and the role of the court.' *Family Law (Bristol)*, 1439–1443.

Herring, J. (2011) 'Farewell welfare.' *Journal of Social Welfare and Family Law 27*, 2, 159–171.

Hindley, N., Ramchandani, P.G. and Jones, D.P.H. (2006) 'Risk factors for recurrence of maltreatment: A systematic review.' *Archives of Disease in Childhood 91*, 9, 744–752.

Holland, S. and Scourfield, J. (2004) 'Liberty and respect in child protection.' *British Journal of Social Work 24*, 1, 17–32.

Holt, K. (2013) 'Territory skirmishes with DIY advocacy in the family courts: A Dickensian misadventure.' *Journal of Family Law 36*, 6, 1123–1131.

Holt, K. (2014a) *Social Work Law.* Palgrave: London.

Holt, K. (2014b) *Exploring the Tensions in Public Law Child Care Proceedings: An Analysis of the Legislative Boundaries of Decision-Making within Pre-proceedings Protocols and the Role of Advocacy in Promoting Justice for Families.* PhD thesis, University of Bradford. Available at https://bradscholars.brad.ac.uk/bitstream/handle/10454/7269/PdF%20Thesis-%20Holt%201.pdf?sequence=1, accessed on 5 March 2016.

Holt, K. and Kelly, N. (2012a) 'Administrative decision making in child-care work: Exploring issues of judgement and decision making in the context of human rights and its relevance for social workers and managers.' *British Journal of Social* Work. DOI: 10.1093/bjsw/bcs168.

Holt, K.E. and Kelly, N. (2012b) 'Rhetoric and reality surrounding care proceedings: Family justice under strain.' *Journal of Social Welfare and Family Law 34*, 2, 155–166.

Holt, K.E. and Kelly, N. (2014a) 'The emperor has no robes: Why are members of the judiciary in the most complex of child-care cases abandoning a sinking ship?' *Journal of Family Law 44*, 10, 1424–1434.

Holt, K. and Kelly, N. (2014b) 'Why parents matter: Exploring the impact of a hegemonic concern with the timetable for the child.' *Child and Family Social Work.* DOI: 10.111/cfs12125.

Holt, K.E. and Kelly, N. (2015a) 'Access to justice: The welfare of children and their families lost in a target focused and cost driven system.' *Journal of Family Law 45*, 2, 167–174.

Holt, K.E. and Kelly, N. (2015b) 'Factors that influence engagement in pre-proceedings practice: Presenting the roles of professionals working within the family justice system through personal narratives.' *Journal of Social Welfare and Family Law*. http://dx.doi.org/10.1080/09649069.2016.1109751.

Holt, K.E. and Kelly, N. (2015c) 'Motivate to mediate – The carrot and stick approach to achieving justice for children and their families within an English legal system.' *International Journal of Family Law 2*, 161–171.

Holt, K.E. and Kelly, N. (2015d) 'What has happened since the Family Justice Review: A brighter future for whom?' *Journal of Family Law 45*, 7, 807–813.

Holt, K.E. and Kelly, N. (2015e) 'When adoption without parental consent breaches human rights: Implications of *Re B-S (Children)* [2013] EWCA Civ 963 on decision making and permanency planning for children.' *Journal of Social Welfare and Family Law 37*, 2, 228–240.

Holt, K.E. and Kelly, N. (2015f) 'When is it too late? An examination of *A and B v Rotherham Metropolitan Borough Council* [2014] EWFC 47.' *Journal of Family Law 45*, 403–410.

Holt, K., Broadhurst, K., Doherty, P. and Kelly, N. (2013a) 'Access to justice for families? Legal advocacy for parents where children are on the "edge of care": An English case study.' *Journal of Social Welfare and Family Law 35*, 12, 1–15.

Holt, K.E., Kelly, N., Broadhurst, K., Doherty, P. and Yeend, E. (2013b) *Liverpool Pre-Proceedings Pilot: Interim Report*. London: Cafcass.

Holt, K., Kelly, N., Broadhurst, K. and Doherty, P. (2014) *Liverpool Pre-Proceedings Pilot: Final Report*. London: Cafcass.

Home Office (1998) *Supporting Families* (Consultation Paper). London: HMSO.

Horwath, J. and Morrison, T. (2001) 'Assessment of Parental Motivation to Change.' In J. Horwath (ed.) *The Child's World: The Comprehensive Guide to Assessing Children in Need*. London: Jessica Kingsley Publishers.

Howe, D. (1997) 'Psychosocial and relationship-based theories for child and family social work: Political philosophy, psychology and welfare practice.' *Child and Family Social Work 2*, 3, 161–169.

Hunt, J., Macleod, A. and Thomas, C. (1999) *The Last Resort: Child Protection, the Courts and the 1989 Children Act*. London: TSO.

Jay, A. (2015) *Independent Inquiry into Child Sexual Exploitation in Rotherham, 1997–2013*. Rotherham: Rotherham Safeguarding Children Board.

Jefferson, G. (2004) 'Glossary of Transcript Symbols with an Introduction.' In G.H. Lerner (ed.) *Conversation Analysis: Studies from the First Generation*. Amsterdam/Philadelphia: John Benjamins.

Jenson, J. (2009) *Diffusing Ideas for After-neoliberalism: The Social Investment Perspective in Europe and Latin America*. Montréal: Université de Montréal.

Jessiman, P., Keogh, P. and Brophy, J. (2009) *An Early Process Evaluation of the Public Law Outline in Family Courts*. Ministry of Justice Research Series 10/09. London: MOJ.

Jones, M. (2014) 'Re B-S and the perils of the "balance sheet" approach.' *Family Law Week*, 28 May 2014.

Jordan, B. and Drakeford, M. (2012) *Social Work and Social Policy under Austerity*. Basingstoke: Palgrave.

Kaganas, F. (1995) 'Partnership under the Children Act 1989: An overview.' In F. Kaganas, M. King and C. Piper (eds) *Legislating for Harmony.* London: Jessica Kingsley Publishers.

Kaganas, F. (2010) 'When it comes to contact disputes, what are family courts for?' *Current Legal Problems 63,* 1, 235– 271.

Kaganas, F., King, M. and Piper, C. (eds) (1995) *Legislating for Harmony: Partnership under the Children Act 1989.* London: Jessica Kingsley Publishers.

Kelly, N. (2002) 'Decision Making in Child Protection Practice.' Unpublished doctoral thesis, University of Huddersfield.

La Valle, I., Payne, L. and Jelicic, H. (2012) *The Voice of the Child in the Child Protection System.* London: NCB.

Laming, The Lord (2009) *The Protection of Children in England: A Progress Report.* Report for the House of Commons. London: TSO.

Lefevre, M. (2010) *Communicating with Children and Young People: Making a Difference.* Social Work in Practice series. Bristol: Policy Press.

Lefevre, M. (2014) 'Learning and development journeys towards effective communication with children.' *Child and Family Social Work.* DOI: 10.1111/cfs.12202.

Legal Services Commission (2011) *Fee Scheme Guidance.* London: HMSO.

Lindley, B. (1994) *Families in Court: Final Report. A Qualitative Study of the Experiences of the Court Process in Care and Supervision Proceedings under the Children Act.* London: Family Rights Group.

Lister, R. (2006) 'Ladder of opportunity or engine of inequality?' *The Political Quarterly 77,* 1, 232–236.

Lonne, B., Parton, N., Thompson, J. and Harries, M. (2009) *Reforming Child Protection.* London & New York: Routledge.

Luckock, B. (2008) 'Adoption support and the negotiation of ambivalence in family policy and children's services.' *Journal of Law and Society 35,* 1, 3–27.

Luckock, B. and Broadhurst, K. (2013) *Adoption Cases Reviewed: An Indicative Study of Process and Practice.* Project Report. London: Department of Education.

Masson, J. (2008) 'Controlling costs and maintaining services – The reform of legal aid fees for care proceedings.' *Child and Family Law Quarterly 20,* 4, 425–448.

Masson, J. (2012) '"I think I do have strategies": Lawyers' approaches to parental engagement in care proceedings.' *Child and Family Social Work 17,* 2, 202–211.

Masson, J. (2014) 'The quality of care proceedings reform.' *Journal of Social Welfare and Family Law 36,* 1, 82–84.

Masson, J. (2015) 'Third (or fourth) time lucky for care proceedings reform?' *Child and Family Law Quarterly 27,* 1, 3–23.

Masson, J.M., Pearce, J.F. and Bader, K.F. (2008) *Care Profiling Study.* MOJ Research Series 4/08. London: MOJ and DCSF.

Masson, J.M., Dickens, J., Bader, K.F. and Young, J. (2013) *'Partnership by Law? The Pre-proceedings Process for Families on the Edge of Care Proceedings'.* Bristol: School of Law, University of Bristol.

Ministry of Justice (2003) *Protocol for Judicial Case Management.* TSO: London.

Ministry of Justice (2008) *Public Law Outline.* London: TSO.

Ministry of Justice (2011a) *Family Justice Review: Final Report.* London: MOJ.

Ministry of Justice (2011b) *Family Justice Review: Interim Report.* London: MOJ.

Ministry of Justice (2013) *Practice Direction 36C – Pilot Scheme: Care and Supervision Proceedings and Other Proceedings Under Part 4 of the Children Act 1989.* London: TSO.

Ministry of Justice (2014a) *Courts and Tribunals Judiciary Response of the Judicial Executive Board to the Justice Committee Inquiry: Civil Legal Aid.* 13 May 2014. London: MOJ.

Ministry of Justice (2014b) *Making the Family Justice System More Effective.* London: MOJ.

Ministry of Justice (2015) *Proposal on the Provision of Court and Tribunal Estate in England and Wales* (Consultation). London: MOJ.

Ministry of Justice and Department for Children, Schools and Families (2009) *Preparing for Care and Supervision Proceedings – A Best Practice Guide.* London: MOJ.

Ministry of Justice and Department for Education (2012) *The Government Response to the Family Justice Review: A System with Children and Families at its Heart.* London: TSO.

Morris, K. (2013) 'Troubled families: Vulnerable families' experiences of multiple service use.' *Child and Family Social Work 18,* 2, 198–206.

Morris, K. and Featherstone, B. (2010) 'Investing in children, regulating parents, thinking family: A decade of tensions and contradictions.' *Social Policy and Society 9,* 4, 557–566.

Muncie, J. (2006) 'Repenalisation and rights: Explorations in comparative youth criminology.' *Howard Journal of Criminal Justice 45,* 1, 42–70.

Munro, E. (2011) *The Munro Review of Child Protection: Final Report – A Child Centred System.* London: Department for Education.

Munro, E. and Ward. H. (2008) 'Balancing parents' and very young children's rights in care proceedings: Decision-making in the context of the Human Rights Act 1998.' *Child and Family Social Work 13,* 2, 227–234.

Nelken, D. (1987) 'The use of "contracts" as a social work technique.' *Current Legal Problems 40,* 1, 207–232.

Neuberger, D. (2013) 'Judges and Policy: A Delicate Balance.' 18 June 2013. London: Institute for Government. Available at https://www.supremecourt.uk/docs/speech-130618.pdf, accessed on 20 December 2015.

Newman, J., Glendinning, C. and Hughes, M. (2008) 'Beyond modernisation? Social care and the transformation of welfare governance.' *Journal of Social Policy 37,* 4, 531–557.

Office for National Statistics (2013) *Focus on: Violent Crime and Sexual Offences, 2011/12.* Statistical Bulletin. Available at http://webarchive.nationalarchives.gov.uk/20160105160709/http://www.ons.gov.uk/ons/dcp171778_298904.pdf, accessed on 30 March 2016.

Ofsted (2011) *Ages of Concern: Learning Lessons from Serious Case Reviews. A Thematic Report of Ofsted's Evaluation of Serious Case Reviews from 1 April 2007 to 31 March 2011.* London: Ofsted.

Ofsted (2012) *Protecting Disabled Children: Thematic Inspection.* London: Ofsted.

Parkinson, L. (1997) *Family Mediation.* London: Sweet and Maxwell.

Parkinson, L. (2005) 'The Future of Family Mediation.' In *Family Meditation* [revised Spanish edition]. Barcelona: Gedisa Editorial.

Parton, N. (2006) *Safeguarding Childhood: Early Intervention and Surveillance in a Late Modern Society.* Basingstoke: Palgrave Macmillan.

Parton, N. (2014a) 'Social work, child protection and politics: Some critical and constructive reflections.' *British Journal of Social Work 44,* 7, 2042–2056.

Parton, N. (2014b) *The Politics of Child Protection: Contemporary Developments and Future Directions.* London: Palgrave Macmillan.

Pearce, J., Masson, J. and Bader, K. (2011) *'Just Following Instructions?' The Representation of Parents in Care Proceedings.* Bristol: School of Law, University of Bristol.

Phelan, T. (2003) *1-2-3 Magic: Effective Discipline for Children 2–12.* Glen Ellyn, IL: Child Management.

Piper, C.D. (2008) 'Will Law Think about Children? Reflections on Youth Matters.' In A. Invernizzi and J. Williams (eds) *Children and Citizenship.* London: Sage Publications.

Radford, L., Corral, S., Bradley, C., Fisher, H. *et al.* (2011) *Child Abuse and Neglect in the UK Today.* London: NSPCC.

Rapoport, A. (1986) *General Systems Theory: Essential Concepts and Applications.* Cambridge, MA: Abacus Press.

Rees, G., Gorin, S., Jobe, A., Stein, M., Medforth, R. and Goswami, H. (2010) *Safeguarding Young People: Responding to Young People Aged 11 to 17 Who Are Maltreated.* London: Children's Society.

Reissman, C. and Quinney, L. (2005) 'Narrative in social work: A critical review.' *Qualitative Social Work 4,* 4, 391–412.

Sabates, R. and Dex, S. (2012) *Multiple Risk Factors in Young Children's Development.* London: Centre for Longitudinal Studies.

Shaw, I., Bell, M., Sinclair, I., Sloper, P. *et al.* (2009) 'An exemplary scheme? An evaluation of the Integrated Children's System.' *British Journal of Social Work 39,* 4, 613–626.

Shaw, M., Broadhurst, K., Harwin, J., Alrouh, B., Kershaw, S. and Mason, C. (2014) 'Recurrent care proceedings: Part 1: Progress in research and practice since the Family Justice Council 6th Annual Debate.' *Family Law (Bristol),* 1284–1287.

Sidebotham, P. (2012) 'What do serious case reviews achieve?' *Archives of Disease in Childhood 97,* 3, 189–192.

Sidebotham, P., Golding, G. and ALSPAC Study Team (2001) 'Child maltreatment in the "children of the nineties": A longitudinal study of parental risk factors.' *Child Abuse and Neglect 25,* 1177–1200.

Sinclair, R. and Bullock, R. (2002) *Learning from Past Experience: A Review of Serious Case Reviews*. London: Department of Health.

Snell, K.D.M. (2006) 'Parish and belonging: community, identity and welfare in England and Wales 1700–1950.' *Journal of British Studies 47*, 2, 436–438.

Stanić, G. (2005) 'Self-Determination in Parent–Child Relationships in Serbia and Montenegro.' In M. Martín-Casals and J. Ribot Igualada (eds) *The Role of Self-Determination in the Modernisation of Family Law in Europe*. Girona: Documenta Universitaria.

Sverdrup, T. (2005) 'European Family Law in Action. Volume III: Parental Responsibilities.' In K. Boele-Woelki, B. Braat and I. Curry-Sumner (eds) *European Family Law in Action. Volume III*. Cambridge: Intersentia.

Swain, P.A. (2009) *In the Shadow of the Law*. Sydney, NSW: Federation Press.

Sykes, J. (2011) 'Negotiating stigma: Understanding mothers' responses to accusations of child neglect.' *Children and Youth Services Review 33*, 3, 448–456.

Teddlie, C. and Tashakkori, A. (eds) (2010) *Sage Handbook of Mixed Methods in Social and Behavioural Research* (2nd edn). Thousand Oaks, CA: Sage.

Thoburn, J., Lewis, A. and Shemmings, D. (1995) *Paternalism or Partnership? The Involvement of Family Members in Child Protection*. London: HMSO.

Todd, A. and Fisher, S. (eds) (1993) *The Social Organisation of Doctor–Patient Communication* (2nd edn). Norwood, NJ: Ablex.

Torsney, P. and Henderson, C. (2013) *The State of the Sector: The Impact of Cuts to Civil Legal Aid on Practitioners and their Clients*. Warwick: University of Warwick.

Treloar, R. and Boyd, S. (2014) 'Family law reform in (Neoliberal) context: British Columbia's new Family Law Act.' *International Journal of Law, Policy and the Family 28*, 1, 77–99.

Tughan, J. (2015) 'Children: Public Law Update (March 2015).' *Family Law Week*, 3 March 2015.

Turney, D. (2005) 'Who Cares? The Role of Mothers in Cases of Child Neglect.' In J. Taylor and B. Daniel (eds) *Child Neglect Practice Issues for Health and Social Care*. London: Jessica Kingsley Publishers.

Tweedale, R. (2015) 'Save Legal Aid, Save Lives.' *Family Law Week*, 24 March 2015.

Wannacott, J. and Watts, D. (2014) *Daniel Pelka Review – Retrospective Deeper Analysis and Progress Report on Implementation of Recommendations*. Independent report commissioned by Coventry Safeguarding Children Board, Coventry.

Wastell, D., White, S., Broadhurst, K., Hall, C., Peckover, S. and Pithouse, A. (2010) 'Children's services in the iron cage of performance management: Street-level bureaucracy and the spectre of Švejkism.' *International Journal of Social Welfare 19*, 3, 310–320.

Welbourne, P. (2008) 'Safeguarding children on the edge of care: Policy for keeping children safe after the Review of the Child Care Proceedings System, Care Matters and the Carter Review of Legal Aid.' *Child and Family Quarterly 20*, 3, 335–358.

Welbourne, P. (2014) 'Time is of the essence: Risk and the Public Law Outline, judicial discretion and the determination of a child's best interests.' *Social Sciences 3*, 3, 584–605.

Wetherell, M. (1998) 'Positioning and interpretative repertoires: Conversation analysis and post-structuralism in dialogue.' *Discourse and Society 9*, 3, 387–412.

White, S. and Broadhurst, K. (2009) 'Raging against the machine.' *Professional Social Work*, January, 8–10.

White, S., Morris, K. and Featherstone, B. (2014) *Re-imaging Child Protection: Towards Humane Social Work with Families*. Bristol: Policy Press.

Wilkins, D. (2013) 'Balancing risk and protective factors: How do social workers and social work managers analyse referrals that may indicate children are at risk of significant harm.' *British Journal of Social Work 45*, 1, 395–411. DOI: 10.1093/bjsw/bct114.

Williams F. (2001) 'In and beyond New Labour: Towards a new political ethic of care.' *Critical Social Policy 21*, 4, 467–493.

Woodhouse, S. (1995) 'Child Protection and Working in Partnership with Parents.' In F. Kaganas (ed.) *Legislating for Harmony*. London: Jessica Kingsley Publishers.

Subject Index

Author Index